EDITH
STEIN

EDITH STEIN

Scholar
Feminist
Saint

FREDA MARY OBEN, Ph D

ALBA · HOUSE   NEW · YORK

SOCIETY OF ST. PAUL, 2187 VICTORY BLVD., STATEN ISLAND, NEW YORK 10314

Library of Congress Cataloging-in-Publication Data

Oben, Freda Mary.
    Edith Stein, scholar, feminist, saint.
        Bibliography: p.
        1. Stein, Edith, 1891-1942.   2. Carmelite Nuns — German
(West) — Biography.   3. Converts, Catholic — Germany
(West) — Biography.   4. Philosophers — Germany (West) —
Biography.   I. Title.
BX4668.S73024   1988   271'.971'024 [B]   87-24178
ISBN 0-8189-0523-9

Designed, printed and bound in the United States of
America by the Fathers and Brothers of the
Society of St. Paul, 2187 Victory Boulevard,
Staten Island, New York 10314, as part of their
communications apostolate.

6 7 8 9 (Current Printing: first digit)

Acknowledgments

Chapter Three, *Spring of the Bitter Valley: Edith Stein and the Holocaust* was originally presented in a slightly different form at the Saint Catherine of Siena Colloquium on Spirituality, "Fires of Hope: 20th Century Spiritual Writers," on Saturday, March 1, 1986 at the Dominican House of Studies in Washington, D.C. It was produced as a tape by Ministr-O-Media, Inc., of Pomfret, Maryland.

Photo Credit: Dr. Freda Mary Oben: 12, 14.
Rev. John Sullivan, O.C.D. (Institute of Carmelite Studies): 1-11, 13, 15.

Table of Contents

EDITH STEIN

CHAPTER ONE

From Atheism to Sainthood:
THE STORY OF EDITH STEIN

The village of Birkenau in Germany received its name in token of the lovely birch trees growing everywhere in such profusion. This pretty little village, emptied of its inhabitants, became an extension of the Auschwitz concentration camp. In the transport of 559 people which arrived there from Holland on August 9, 1942, there were two sisters, Edith and Rosa Stein.

Because of the horrible traveling conditions, many had already died in transit. Many survivors had psychologically broken down. Edith was still wearing her Carmelite habit, and so conspicuous was she by her appearance and manner that one of the guards later testified that he turned to another guard and said, "That one is sane, anyway."[1]

The people were ordered to form lines of five. The SS doctor selected 295 persons he considered fit for work. The others, 264 including Edith and Rosa, were driven in lorries to huts in the nearby woods where they were told to undress for showers and delousing.

During this summer of 1942, two farm cottages were being used for the gassing—a red and a white one. It is believed that Edith was led to the latter. A former guard of Auschwitz writes: "Nobody could have thought it credible that in those insignificant little houses as many people had perished as would have filled a city."[2]

These victims went to their death completely duped. They were disarmed by the lovely pastoral scene and the matter-of-fact small talk of the "Sonderkommandos" and SS men. Those who did show panic were shoved inside quickly. If any became hysterical, they were immediately forced to the back of the cottage and shot.

The cottages were windowless. As soon as the strong, air-tight doors were bolted down by screws, Zyklon B poison gas was discharged through vents in the ceilings. In about fifteen to twenty minutes it was all over.

In the autobiography of the camp commander, Rudolf Hoess, we find the following passage:

> During the summer of 1942, the bodies were still being placed in mass graves. Towards the end of the summer, however, we started to burn them, at first on wood pyres bearing some 2,000 corpses, and later in pits together with bodies previously buried . . . Bodies were burnt in pits day and night, continuously . . . By the end of November all the mass graves had been emptied.[3]

In March of 1984, I stood by the remains of the white cottage which is flanked by a large birch tree. Several of the former mass graves are still discernible near the cottage. The pits are marked by large white crosses. My guide told me that the ashes of the cremations had been used as fertilizer for the surrounding fields or else simply dumped into the nearby pond or the Vistula River. We walked to the edge of this pond. The calcium remains along its edges can be clearly seen. He retrieved a fistful of small bits of white bone from the mud and placed it in my hand. Time stopped for me.

I had come to the camp, now called the Auschwitz Museum, to do research on Edith Stein, the famous German philosopher, educator and feminist. After a two-hour interview with the camp director, I was shown about the camp by a young man from the camp Archives and then given material and photographs from the Archives. I am indebted to them for this new and authentic description of her death. Yet there are no formal records of Edith, because the prisoners designated for death right from the train were never registered.

I then went to find the beginnings of Edith's life in Wroclaw, Poland. Formerly known as Breslau in Silesia, in Germany, this lovely medieval city of religion and culture was ceded back to Poland at the end of the Second World War. Edith was born the eleventh child, the seventh surviving, to Siegfried and Augusta Stein on October 12, 1891 in a small house on Kohlenstrasse. The parents had come from Lublintz just a half year before her birth to seek a better living.

In that year, this date fell on the Jewish Day of Atonement, "Yom Kippur." Edith explains in her autobiography that this correlation of events was so important to her mother that it was the paramount reason why her mother held her so dear. She describes another tender association. On a very hot day in July, Mrs. Stein was holding a mere twenty-one month old Edith as Mr. Stein made his farewells: he was going on a long trek to a distant forest for his lumber business. Edith called after her father from her mother's arms, and this moment was the last memory Mrs. Stein retained of her husband, for he was to die of sunstroke that very day.

Edith confesses that she was a headstrong child. At times merry and saucy, she was at other times most naughty and willful; in fact, she became infuriated when she could not have her own way. Her mother now took charge of the lumber business, and the elder sisters took turns caring for Edith and her sister Erna who was also quite small. At times her sister Else resorted to locking a naughty Edith in a dark place. Edith writes that when, lying in her tantrum on the floor she saw this coming, she would deliberately make herself rigid, and once locked in, did not submit to her fate but lay screaming and kicking the door until she was liberated, usually by her mother.

Although she worked, Mrs. Stein remained the center of the home and for Edith was always an image of the proverbial woman of faith, courage and industry. Her mother went to synagogue with the elder brothers and sisters on the Jewish high holy days. However, the business remained open on Saturdays, and prayers in the home were recited in German and not Hebrew.

She was a precocious child who, according to her sister Erna, was indoctrinated into the field of literature when she was only four years old. Erna writes:

> One of my earliest memories is of my eldest brother Paul carrying Edith around the room in his arms and singing student songs to her, or showing her pictures in a History of Literature and lecturing her on Schiller, Goethe, etc. She had a tremendous memory and forgot nothing of all this.[4]

Edith writes of herself as a seven year-old experiencing a secret, inner life which she was unable to express. She envisioned a radiant life of happiness and glory. (This inner life which she keeps quietly hidden within her is, of course, what she develops so beautifully in her vocation as a contemplative. She could not readily talk about this interiority even when she was older; she was known to be reserved.) Reason had taken hold and her disposition changed. Temper tantrums were no longer possible, for she felt shame in seeing others lose their tempers. At a very early age she attained self-mastery and the quality of trustful submission.[5] We shall see this beautiful bent of her character later in her complete surrender to the will of God.

But at the age of fifteen, a dual blight hit her soul. The child who had wheedled her way into school on her sixth birthday—even though it was the middle of the semester—announced suddenly to her mother that she did not want to continue school! And she writes, moreover, "I dropped prayer consciously and by my own free decision."[6] She went to help her sister Else in Hamburg with the children and house. But six months later, she informed her mother that she intended to return to school and then go on to college. Edith was to be among the first group of women entering a university. She had evidently discovered at her sister's that domesticity was not exactly her cup of tea!

When she was seventeen, she started to attend the Girls' High School in Breslau. That same year, in 1908, another teenager, the nineteen-year-old Adolf Hitler, had already failed the entrance exam to the academy of arts and was reading anti-Semitic newspapers in Linz.

During her last years in high school, the Stein family moved into the spacious house which they called "the Villa" at 38 Michaelisstrasse, now called Nowowiejska. The architectural beauty of this house is evident. The large two-story brick building is now covered with grey plaster. It is divided equally in two parts. I counted nineteen windows in the front alone!

The spacious street adjoins a park where children play by the lake. Nearby, the tower of St. Michael's Church looms high, the church to which she was to steal away quietly in future years for the 6 a.m. Mass. I am sure she heard the chimes tolling even in her young years, but then she was deep in the bosom of her family with loads of aunts, uncles, cousins, and joy. This strong love for her family and theirs for her was to form an integral part of her nature and helped to determine her fate. At this time, an orphaned Hitler was hiding in Vienna and dodging conscription by the Austrian army.

Her inability to pray, what she termed her atheism, continued through her first two years at the University of Breslau, where she enrolled in 1911. Edith was registered in the Department of Experimental Psychology, a branch of the Philosophy Department. She writes that at that time, 1911-13, the existence of the human soul was not acknowledged in the field of psychology.

An incident which occurred in 1912 reveals her deep concern for humanity and its disorders. She was twenty, and had just read a novel painting in most frightening colors the link between student alcoholism and amorality. She reacted violently. Nauseated, she lost her trust in humanity and was submerged under a pain of cosmic weight. It is an early instance of her concept of co-responsibility which we find developed to perfection in her adulthood.

She was cured, she writes, by attending a concert of Bach (whom she calls her "Liebling"—that is, "darling" or "favorite") where Luther's hymn, "A Mighty Fortress is our God" was also sung. She responded with rising joy to the third verse:

Though hordes of devils fill the land
All threatening to devour us
We tremble not, unmoved we stand
They cannot overpower us.[7]

Her cosmic pain fell away. Certainly, the world was bad. But if she and her friends stuck together, they could get rid of all the devils! Note that she said "friends" rather than "God"—the protagonist against the devil in Luther's song.

This was shortly before her 21st birthday, and Edith has confessed that she was unable to believe in a personal God until she was 21. At that time, she transferred from the University of Breslau to the University of Göttingen. At Breslau she had intended to write a thesis in the Department of Experimental Psychology but was definitely disenchanted. The light awaiting her intellect and soul was elsewhere; it beckoned to her through her reading of the second volume of Husserl's *Logical Investigations*.

There is no doubt that this was the immediate cause of her decision to study under Husserl at the University of Göttingen. But although she considered herself an intellectual in search of truth, her transfer to Göttingen can be seen only in the light of God's providence; granted her unique spiritual hunger and potential, God lifted her out and brought her to the decidedly religious influence there. It is also of particular significance that she would find herself there in a circle of Jewish intellectuals—Husserl, Reinach and Scheler in particular—who in one way or another had become Christians.

Edith's description of the old university town of Göttingen, of the Department of Philosophy and its Philosophical Circle is quite charming. She describes her arrival there in the summer of 1913: "Dear old Göttingen! I don't believe that anyone who did not study there between 1905 and

1914, during the short springtime of the Göttingen phenomenology school, could ever imagine what that name conjures up for us."[8]

There is a plaque on the house where she roomed: *Edith Stein, Philosopher, 1913-1916*. I walked past St. Albani Church from which she had heard the Angelus ring three times daily, then on to the marketplace to admire the Goose Girl fountain which still stands there. I stopped for coffee at the Kron und Lanz coffee shop of which Edith speaks, and then I walked through the building which housed the philosophy seminars she attended.

She loved nature and took frequent hikes and picnics with her friends. I followed her route to Nikolausberg almost expecting to come upon the "three wind-stripped trees" which had reminded her of Golgotha—a strange image to come to the mind of this young Jewish atheist! I sat on the edge of a wheat field filled with pink and white flowers, and in that solitude and silence I felt the deep love which Edith had for the German land.

Her love for art, music and literature drew her on longer journeys. She climbed the hill from Eisenach to Wartburg Castle where the Middle High German poets had written, where Martin Luther translated the Bible, and where St. Elizabeth of Hungary had lived. Years later, she was to capture this saint beautifully in an essay. She went to Weimar to pay her respects to her childhood idols—Goethe and Schiller. Her compassionate heart was moved by the "miserable little room in which Schiller died." I, too, visited Eisenach and Weimar (now in East Germany), but I must confess I did not climb that huge hill to Wartburg Castle as she did—I took a cab!

Edith gives a minute description of the Göttingen Philosophy Circle, many of whose names are world-famous: Adolf Reinach, Theodor Conrad and Hedwig Martius,

Dietrich von Hildebrand, Alexander Koyré, Fritz Frankfurter and Fritz Kaufmann. "But," she writes, "the one who most deeply impressed me was Hans Lipps." He was two years older than she was, and was such an ardent philosopher that one time, in a heated discussion, he emptied his cigar into the sugar bowl! Edith had a genuine attachment for him, which was broken off. He died in World War II.

But the star of this Circle was Edmund Husserl. Born in 1859, a Jew, he had been baptized in a Lutheran church on his 27th birthday. "When Edith introduced herself he asked her whether she had read any of his works. She confessed to having perused the whole second volume of his *Logical Investigations*. He told her that this was a truly heroic feat, and required no other credentials for her admission."[9]

Husserl had established the new discipline of phenomenology, and this was a tremendously new world for Edith. It was an entry into a religious ambiance peopled by intellectuals who had a deep spirituality. Many of these people, as I mentioned, were Jewish. Hedwig Conrad-Martius writes that there is an affinity between the Jewish radical spirit and the discipline of phenomenology.[10]

Husserl always recognized a debt to Thomas Aquinas, admitting that his discipline "converges towards Thomism and prolongs Thomism."[11] Ontology was now given new respect because Husserl, in his search for truth, recognized not only the reality of this seemingly visible objective world but also the reality of the transcendent. And Edith knew that here was something with which she had to come to grips. This intellectual who had heretofore felt herself secure within the barriers of her mind now recognized that there was a new world she had to understand.

Edith had changed universities in the pursuit of truth. She considered herself an atheist, yet she was able to write later that whoever searches for truth is actually searching for

God whether he acknowledges this or not. As a young girl of twenty, she had great confidence in her own intellect. No one could tell her anything! But she tended to be critical toward other people, and her wit was apt to be caustic. Now, when she came to the University of Göttingen, she found that the great intellects there were investigating the essence and structure of supernatural truths which they regarded as being just as real as other phenomena.

Edith's friend, the philosopher Peter Wust explains: ". . . from the very beginning, there seemed to be in the intention of the new philosophical perspective something hidden which was completely mysterious, a searching back for objectivity to the sacredness of being, to the purity and chasteness of things, 'of the thing in itself.' "

Hedwig Conrad-Martius described the existing challenge in these words: "Can the scientist even take the responsibility not to come to terms with the problem of the existence of a thing which has suddenly appeared in a very impressionable sense as able to exist?"[12]

Edith's atheism was confronted by the phenomenological ideal of objective clarity. Revelation became a viable object of scrutiny. She studied the Greek philosophers, but under Husserl's influence also turned to medieval Scholasticism. And at some time in a linguistics course, she studied the Lord's Prayer in Old Gothic and was very affected by it.

She was particularly challenged by the spiritual thrust of two professors, Max Scheler and Adolf Reinach.

At this time, Scheler was in the throes of a renewed Catholic fervor. Edith writes that he influenced the students more than Husserl did. Scheler did so especially through his text, *The Formalistic Principle in Ethics and the Non-Formal Ethic of Value*.

One wonders if what she describes as Adolf Reinach's "personal goodness" may have encouraged Edith in her deep absorption with the person and the human spirit. This keen interest found its fuller development in her later identity as a Christian and a Carmelite.

In her doctoral thesis, *On the Problem of Empathy*, she investigated the "psycho-physical individual." This was her first attempt to treat the major theme of all her writings, the structure of the human spirit.

This study also reveals a growing sense of responsibility as a member of the human family. She analyzes not only the self, the "I," but is interested in the relationship of the "I" to "the other." She asks, "How do I know what is going on in the other person? What is foreign experience in its givenness?" She believes that the experience of "the other" cannot be duplicated as it occurs originally, but that if we put ourselves in the place of the other and immerse ourselves in the circumstances of his situation, we gain in knowledge of his experience.[13]

While Edith was involved in this search for truth, which she describes as a prayer in itself, Hitler was finally found in Munich in 1914 and escorted to the Austrian Consulate. That fatal summer he willingly joined the German army for the war. He was to claim later that "the First World War taught him more about the real 'problems of life' than thirty years at a university could have done."[14]

Reinach also enlisted that summer. Edith, after passing the state exams in history, philosophy and German, served as a Red Cross nurse for six months (April-September, 1915) at the Weisskirchen Epidemic Hospital in Moravia. She nursed soldiers of the Austrian army infected with spotted fever, dysentery and cholera.

We find here a striking instance on her independence. She writes: "My mother opposed me vigorously . . . she declared energetically, 'You will never go with my consent!'

and I answered with equal determination, 'Then I shall have to go without your consent.' "[15]

After this, she taught for eight months at the high school in Breslau where she herself had studied. Then, on August 3, 1916, she made the trip to Husserl to receive her doctorate "summa cum laude." He had been given a chair in phenomenology at Freiburg University, and it is a recognition of her singular genius that of all his students, many of whom were to become famous, Husserl now invited Edith to come as his first assistant in October. She stayed for eighteen months.

Edith taught Husserl's beginning students, referring to them humorously as her "philosophical kindergarten." Her main task, however, was to get Husserl's manuscripts in order for publication. She had the formidable task of transcribing his notes from Gabelsberger shorthand, elaborating them if necessary, and editing them. Her colleague, Roman Ingarden, explains how difficult this really was since Husserl's creativity compelled him to write in bursts, in fragments, but never to reread or revise his manuscripts. It is due to Edith's efforts that it was later possible to publish Husserl's works of this period.[16]

But her stay in Freiburg was not just a round of drudgery. She enjoyed many long hikes in the area with her friends—in the city itself and in the surrounding Black Forest. On these trips she liked to discuss such favorite authors as Stefan George, Goethe and Gottfried Keller.

I have been told by Edith's friends and family that she herself was particularly rich in the faculty of empathy that she had written about—of understanding other persons and relating to them. I believe that it was this particular gift which enabled her to have an experience which she tells us marks the beginning of her real conversion.

Adolf Reinach died at the front in November, 1917. His funeral was in Göttingen in December. Edith went to see her friend, his widow Anna Reinach. To her surprise she found a woman at peace rather than a despairing widow. Anna was able to stand up to the blow because of her strong Christian faith. Adolf Reinach had become a Protestant at the front, and Anna had followed him into the Church. Edith's ability to recognize the workings of another soul gave her at this time a real awareness, a living recognition and knowledge of the power of the cross.

The testimony of two priests bears witness to the importance of this visit in Edith's conversion.

Father John Nota writes that she described this incident to him some time before her arrest, and that she still felt the dynamic impression made on her by Mrs. Reinach. Anna was able to console Edith rather than be consoled by her because of her faith in a loving God.[17]

Father Johannes Hirschmann, in a letter of May 3, 1950 to the Mother Superior at the Cologne Carmel, writes the following:

> Sister Teresia Benedicta herself distinguished between the cause of her conversion to Christianity from the cause of her entrance to the Catholic Church . . . The most decisive reason for her conversion to Christianity was, as she told me, the way and manner in which her friend Mrs. Reinach made her offer in the power of the mystery of the cross after her husband died at the front during the First World War.[18]

We can see here again that Edith's great gift of relating to people allowed her to experience the essence of the Christian faith. But all this required a period of gestation: it was to be another five years before her decision.

During the time that Edith was editing Husserl's works, she had also been writing articles herself: "Psychic Causality," "The Individual and Community," and "The State."

"Psychic Causality" investigates the "psycho-physical individual" again—but, most important, she analyzes the interrelationship of the person with others in terms of community. There is a beautiful passage in this work which seems to reveal Edith's own inner life at the time. She describes a state of "resting in God": the person surrenders himself and relinquishes all efforts of mind and will; this receptivity is rewarded by new life—"spiritual rebirth" which frees him from all care. Edith writes that this faculty of receptivity is built into the structure of the human being.

In "The Individual and Community" she continues to analyze interrelationships as she investigates the nature of community and compares its structure to that of the person.

Edith's last purely phenomenological work, "The State," furthers her searchings into community as she probes into the nature of the state, its concepts of justice, and even its relationship to values such as religion. In high school, Edith had campaigned as a suffragette; now, in 1918, she canvassed for the German Democratic Party. This political interest led her to write this study.

These three works were published in the *Jahrbuch für Philosophie und phänomenologische Forschung* and represent her purely phenomenological as distinct from her Thomist works.[19]

Edith left her post with Husserl in the fall of 1918 and returned to Breslau, where she continued to write.

Attempts to get another university position failed even with a letter of unqualified recommendation from Husserl, probably because there were few women teaching then in the universities. Another letter was written around this time. In 1919, Hitler wrote to a military officer presenting the views of the German Workers' Party concerning the Jews. In this, his first political manifesto, he lists the "crimes" of the Jews and holds out, as the final objective, the removal of all Jews from their midst.[20]

During the next three years, the dramatic trauma of Edith's conversion developed. When she wrote the essay "Plant Soul, Animal Soul, Human Soul," it seemed to her friends that she had already accepted the Christian faith.[21] Indeed, from Father Hirschmann's letter we know that Edith wanted to become a Christian since the time of her visit to Anna Reinach, but that she did not know which denomination to join. Many of her friends had become Protestants.

She finally decided to enter the Catholic Church after reading St. Teresa of Avila's autobiography. She had been prepared for this by the fervent Catholicism of Max Scheler.

This happened during a prolonged visit to the home of her good friend Hedwig Conrad-Martius in the summer of 1921. Many members of the Göttingen Philosophy Circle still came there from time to time to help gather fruit and to talk philosophy. Hedwig describes the religious crisis that she and Edith were undergoing during that visit: "It was as if we were both walking on a narrow mountain ridge, aware that God's call was imminent." She writes that Edith, always reserved, was at this time intensely quiet.[22]

Her friends having gone out one evening, Edith was left to entertain herself with a book. By chance, she picked up a German translation of St. Teresa of Avila's autobiography and did not close the book until dawn. She tells us herself that she said then, "This is the truth."[23] So convinced was she of the truth of St. Teresa's experience that she had to acknowledge the source of that experience as Truth itself.

I think that because of Edith's gift of being able to identify with another person, she was able to grasp not only the nature of Teresa's religious life but its meaning. She committed herself totally to the saint's admonition to live in surrender and humility.

That very morning, she went directly to buy a Catholic catechism and a missal. On January 1, 1922, she was baptized at St. Martin's Church in Bergzabern. This lovely church nestling in the foothills is now devoted to her memory. Cards of the church are issued bearing her name. A street by the church is called Edith Stein Strasse. The new youth building was constructed in her honor—the Edith Stein House. The new altar, made in the shape of an unsymmetrical T, is not only the symbol of the crucified Christ, but is also a sign of the name Teresia Benedicta a Cruce, Teresa the Cross, Edith's name as a religious.

When Father Breitling, who baptized Edith, died. Blessed by, both the Jewish and Christian communities attended his funeral. All of this can be found in the *Festschrift* issued by that church.

I was lucky enough to stand one day before the font where she was baptized. On the wall, by the font, there is a plaque dedicated to her. It depicts the scene from 1 Kings 19:17. A loaf of bread and jug of water have been placed at the feet of the sleeping Elijah by the angel who bids him: "Get up and eat or the journey will be too long for you." The *Festschrift* suggests that it is the heavenly bread awaiting Edith at the baptismal font, the Eucharist, which alone enabled her to ascend the Mount Horeb of her life through the gas chamber, where she died for her people and her faith.[24]

After her baptism, Edith's whole life changed. This recognized intellectual retired for eight years to a quiet Dominican school in Speyer, St. Magdalene's. She taught high school girls, novices and nuns preparing to teach. She followed the evangelical counsels of poverty, chastity and obedience, and we are told that she accepted little reimbursement other than food, lodging and clothes made for her by the nuns. She had wanted to become a religious immediately after her baptism, but her spiritual director did not permit this because of her prominence as a laywoman and to avoid a further blow to her mother.

She read the office daily, and the psalms were especially beloved by her. She had a very close tie not only to Scripture and the breviary, but to the whole liturgy of the Church.

Always of a very calm nature, she became perfectly balanced and recollected. Formerly, she had been described as "deliciously mischievous" and even "witty almost to the point of malice." She retained her gift of laughter (she could laugh till the tears ran down her face), but she now made herself the object of humor, telling funny stories about herself and her family. Her manner became gentle, patient, modest and humble. Always loving, she now seemed holy.

Jacques Maritain writes, "How can one describe the purity, the light which shone from Edith Stein at the time of her conversion, the total generosity which one felt in her and which was to bear fruit in martyrdom?"[25]

One of her students at St. Magdalene's has testified: "The most fundamental trait of her character was surely a warm love that could penetrate into another's mind, suffering with him, and helping him as only a Christ-centered saint is able to do."[26]

Edith was able to write in *Finite and Eternal Being* that the resurrected Christ is the model and guide for all human formation. In 1921, Hitler was proclaimed leader of the National German Workers' Party. When writing *Mein Kampf* in prison after his unsuccessful putsch, he presented his concept of the Aryan as the true image of God, the highest form of humanity—and the Jew as the exact opposite.

Now Edith realized that her intellectual work could indeed serve her faith. She wanted to study the intellectual foundation of Catholicism and turned to St. Thomas Aquinas. Through him she learned that her intellect was a means of giving herself to God.

Aquinas writes of "This light in which we human beings contemplate truth . . . the light of grace and the light of glory . . ." Through the clear luminosity of her writings, Edith exemplifies that "This light is not only placed in each human learner directly by God Himself, it is also by its very nature a created participation in that supernal light which God Himself is."[27]

Canon Schwind of the Cathedral in Speyer became her revered spiritual director. He said of Edith laughingly one day that all she wanted to do was talk theology and more theology: theology was her spiritual food! He introduced her to the Jesuit philosopher-theologian Erich Przywara, at whose suggestion she translated into German Cardinal Newman's *Letters and Journals* (1801-1845) and *The Idea of a University*[28] and St. Thomas Aquinas' *De Veritate* (*On Truth*).[29] This was the first adequate translation into German of Aquinas' text. Her two-volume edition of it made her famous, for it was a brilliant phenomenological commentary as well as a translation.

During these years at Speyer, Edith also worked on *Potenz und Akt* (*Potency and Act*), the embryo of her greatest philosophical work, *Endliches und Ewiges Sein* (*Finite and Eternal Being*).[30] On Husserl's seventieth birthday in 1929, she contributed an essay to a comparative study, *Husserl's Phenomenology and the Philosophy of St. Thomas Aquinas.*[31] This was a most noted work in the new interrelationship of the two schools of thought.

In the United States, acknowledgment is still to be given to Edith's singular philosophical contribution. She was placed historically at a crossroad of the two disciplines, and because of her unique spiritual and intellectual makeup, she has made a vital, enduring contribution to the trend of twentieth century thought.

She had made great strides in scholarship; let us also note here that during these years at Speyer, her personality was undergoing a great transformation.

She had taken the three private vows (yet so intense was her prayer life that she was apt to stay all night in the chapel strictly against the wishes of her spiritual director!). She termed God "The Master Educator" and she was a very good student. Her critical, even caustic bent had been replaced by the spiritual maternity she was to consider woman's greatest gift whether married or single. Her colleagues and students describe her as gentle, patient, modest, loving, humble, happy, lovable, serene, balanced, charitable and holy. She taught that Christ is the perfect model and Gestalt of all personality, and on this she, too, was formed.

In order to find the right perspective for the education of girls and women, she turned to an analysis of woman's nature and vocation. At this time few were interested in gearing the educational system, which was strictly masculine, to the feminine psyche. She challenged the system by her analysis of woman's unique nature and intrinsic value. She gave her first lecture on this topic in 1928.

And she was the first to reveal the link between woman's nature and religious education. She shows the motivation for such religious education as placed in the very nature of the student. Borrowing an image from St. Thomas, she describes the image of God planted as a seed in the human soul: the seed comes to development by the supernatural aid of grace and the natural help of education—plus, of course, the student's own inner dedication. And this full development of personality implies a wholeness of the person because it is the whole person that is needed for God's service. This requires a balanced development of all physical and psychical powers.

In the lectures that comprise *Die Frau (The Woman)*, from which I am now taking this material, Edith presents an ontology of woman—a study of her being, nature and role proper to happiness.[32] Basic to this ontology is her belief that the human species is a dual one: masculine and feminine. She writes that it is the spiritual essence of man and of woman which determines sexual differentiation.

She finds that woman's vocation is threefold: human, individual, and feminine; the fulfillment of one of these vocations depends on the fulfillment of the other two. She sees woman's unique strength in a spiritual maternity which should be exercised through her professions and which represents her femininity regardless of marital status. She upholds the Church's ideal of marriage; the family should always come first for the woman. Yet she claims that as long as children are properly cared for by loving people, the mother is free to exercise her profession—unless it does, indeed, make problems. She believes that woman's nature best qualifies her for certain professions but that, actually, there is no work performed by a man that a woman cannot do!

Yet the woman differs from the man in the relationship of body to soul and in the relationship of her faculties. She is emotion-centered and thus requires intellectual training to develop objectivity. The woman's view is personal—geared towards the person and relationships, and she is driven to develop herself and those about her to a total humanity. Objectivity is also needed to help her avoid a hyper-feminine personal attitude which is apt to make her a nuisance. The essence of the pedagogical goal is to teach her to relate properly to others and to understand the world so that she can better serve.

The justice of the cause of feminism is evidenced by the singular fact that a woman of such holiness as Edith Stein was a feminist. Indeed, by 1932 she was recognized as the intellectual leader of Catholic feminism in Europe. She delivered lectures constantly, which later became *Die Frau*, for the League of Catholic Women and the Association of Catholic Women Teachers. These groups actually formed the Catholic Women's Movement. She became their "voice," speaking at their annual conventions, acting as their advisor in plans of reform and in discussions with government officials.

She advocated that Catholic thought must meet the challenging questions of the time: sexual problems, teachings on marriage and motherhood, woman's vocation, etc.

> The traditional Catholic handling of these questions or, indeed, the traditional disregard for them could and should be reformed if it is to meet the challenging questions of the time.
>
> The setup of a genuinely Catholic broad-minded approach to marriage and sexuality and the educational principles to be derived from this should therefore be considered as an urgent problem in contemporary education. This means the education of all youth, including young girls.[33]

She rallied Catholic women to get involved. The following lines are from Edith Stein's address to a group of Catholic university women in Switzerland.

> Let's get to the point. . . . Do we grasp social problems,
> the burning problems of today? Do they concern us
> also? Or are we waiting until others find some solution
> or until we are submerged by the billows of chaos? Is
> such an attitude worthy of an academic woman? Must
> we not try to help in deed as well as in thought? . . . . We
> must get in touch with the social ferment of the masses
> and understand their physical and spiritual needs I
> have reached the core of a burning question. . . . Are we
> familiar with the work of the adversary? In the mine
> fields of today's society, can we justify looking back-
> wards continuously while our adversary wages war
> against our views?[34]

We must not forget that Edith was attempting to
counteract the growing Nazi ideology which would reduce
woman to "children, kitchen and church." She urged,
rather, that it is the mission of the twentieth century woman
in a sick society to act as "healthy, energetic spores supplying
healthy energy to the entire national body."[35] But she cannot help others to be whole unless she is a whole person
herself. Against the Nazi ideology which subjected woman
completely to the man's dictates, she urged that women be
trained in value judgments so that they can understand the
world in which they must serve and relate properly to
others.

But she was in too much demand as a speaker, so in 1931
she left her teaching duties at Speyer. At Breslau, she continued to work on *Potency and Act*. Attempts to secure a
teaching post at the University of Freiburg failed, although
her former fellow student and colleague, Martin Heidegger
now held the chair there in phenomenology. In fact, she felt
herself treated by him with considerable ill-will. This is not
surprising in light of the fact that at the time Heidegger was

a strong supporter of the Nazis.[36] Then, in 1932, she accepted an important post at the German Institute for Scientific Pedagogy in Münster.

On September 12th of that year, she participated in a conference held in Juvisy, France by the Thomistic Society. She was the only woman invited to attend. Although Daniel Feuling, O.S.B. gave the paper, a reading of that day's proceedings reveals that Edith made a considerable impact. Professor Rosenmölh writes:

> The discussion was dominated entirely by Edith Stein. Certainly she had the best understanding of Husserl, having been for years his assistant in Freiburg, but she developed her thoughts with such clarity, in French when necessary, that she made an extraordinarily strong impression on this learned company of scholars.[37]

Among "this learned company" were Maritain, Koyré, Gilson and Berdiaev. A letter of the following November indicates that she apparently visited with the Maritains in Mendon at the time of the conference in Juvisy: she recalls the day with joy and thanks him for sending her a copy of his book *Degrees of Knowledge*.

Another letter written at this time to a religious in Speyer expresses Edith's growing difficulty of living in the secular world. Her interiority had developed so strongly that she feared she was projecting a quality troubling to the other women teachers. The innermost part of her being had become her world. She was to explain this in a line found in *Finite and Eternal Being*: ". . . those who live the *interior life* have always experienced being drawn into their innermost parts by that which draws more strongly than the total exterior world: the invasion of a new, forceful, higher life—

the supernatural, divine life."[38] Edith was suffering for she, indeed, had a vocation as a contemplative.

On January 30, 1933, Adolf Hitler became Reich Chancellor of Germany. Edith's Jewish presence was now an embarrassment at the Institute. Although she stayed there throughout the summer, her last lecture was on February 25th. She writes of these last days in Münster: ". . . now on a sudden it was luminously clear to me that once again God's hand lay heavy on His people, and that the destiny of this people was my own."[39] On April 1, 1933, an anti-Jewish boycott was put in effect throughout Germany.

We have now come to the turning point of Edith Stein's life. Clearly, she foresaw the danger which awaited both Jews and Christians. She tried to obtain a private audience with Pope Pius XI to urge that he write an encyclical on behalf of the Jews. When this failed, she wrote a letter to the Pope which was personally delivered by her spiritual advisor, Abbot Raphael Walzer of the Benedictine Abbey at Beuron. In this letter, she warned the Pope that what was happening to the Jews would then happen to the Catholics.

She knew, then, full well the reality of the coming evil. Indeed, Edith's entreaty for action by the Pope as early as the spring of 1933 is so conspicuous in its singularity that historians have noted it as such. We ask: why did she not flee the country as other German Jews were doing? In fact, just that past November she herself had been thinking of going to work in London. And in that month of crisis, April, she was given an opportunity to teach in South America where she would have been with her brother Arno. Instead, she chose the cross.

She has described this crisis in her essay "The Road to Carmel." She writes: "I spoke to our Savior and told him that I knew it was His Cross which was now being laid on the Jewish people. Most of them did not understand it; but those who did understand must accept it willingly in the name of all."[40]

She spent thirteen straight hours of prayer at the St. Ludgeri Church in Münster. I have seen a beautiful plaque dedicated to her there on a wall by a large iron cross. It commemorates those hours of prayer because it was then that she made her great decision to enter Carmel. It was her belief that the Carmelite order excels in a free and joyous participation in Christ's redemptive action. And it was the intention of her innermost being to offer up her prayer and life in reparation for both Jew and Nazi, for the persecutor as well as the persecuted.

Now, this would come very hard to ordinary people like us, no doubt. But let us consider her own words: "Saints who are determined to confidently maintain a courageous love for their enemies have experienced that they have the freedom to so love . . . their behavior is led by supernatural love."[41] Her intention to pray for the Nazis was in keeping with St. John of the Cross who writes: "God sustains and is present substantially in every soul, even that of the worst sinner."[42]

Three weeks after her decision to enter Carmel, she wrote again to the Maritains. Since her last letter to them seven months prior, her whole world had changed. Yet, she said nothing of her hopes for Carmel, telling them only of the termination of her post and asking them not to fear for her because God works all things to the good.

Edith writes to another friend that she believes this friend would want to take upon herself the excess of misery and pain being experienced by so many if only she understood their despair. As all saints have done through time, Edith had set herself on God's side to fight the sins and disorders which were causing this terrible misery, pain and despair. Her weapons were prayer and the face of love. And what sadness she must have felt over this misery, not only as a Jew but as a Christian—for, after all, it was the so-called "Christians" who were among the brutal oppressors. She believed that only the Passion of Christ could save the world, and she wanted a share in that. The Jewish girl born on the holy Jewish Day of Atonement understood well what redemption is.

Yet Edith's anguish was intensified by her family's lack of understanding. If her conversion had been most painful to them, her entrance into Carmel in 1933, at the very onset of their persecution, was unbelievable. There was a touching incident at this time involving Edith and her niece "Susel," and they have both described it.

Susan was at that time twelve years old, and she had heard much talk. She saw her grandmother suffering over the certainty of never seeing Edith again. Her grandmother was eighty-four years old and no longer traveled, and Edith was to be fully cloistered.

Edith writes of this meeting with Susan: " 'Why are you doing this now?' she asked . . . I gave her my reasons as I would to an adult. She listened thoughtfully and understood."[43] Susan, however, describes it differently in a lovely little essay, "Erinnerungen an Meine Tante Edith Stein" (Reminiscences of my Aunt Edith Stein):

> It was characteristic of my aunt that she did not ridicule my words or answer me condescendingly. She was serious and attentive; she said she did not consider her step as a betrayal; she was leaving no one in the lurch. Her entrance into Carmel did not guarantee her any safety and would not eliminate the actual world outside. She would always be a part of her family and always remain part of the Jewish people, even as a nun.[44]

But Susan adds, "A cleft existed between her and her family which could not be reconciled although, on the other hand, we could not stop loving her."[45]

This was all part of Edith's personal, unique cross. Her redemptive role was unique in its duality: as a Jew, she suffered for her people, and as a Christian, she underwent the passion of Christ her Lord, united to Him as He suffered for Jews and Gentiles alike.

On October 14th, 1933, two days after her forty-second birthday, she entered the Mary Queen of Peace Carmel in Cologne. This was the eve of the feastday of its founder. St. Teresa of Avila had led her home.

Her investiture took place the following April and was attended by many people of repute in the world of philosophy, religion and academia. She adopted as her religious name Teresia Benedicta a Cruce, Teresa Blessed by the Cross. But there is also a correlation to the Benedictine Abbey at Beuron and its abbot, Raphael Walzer, who had been her spiritual director. She had a great love for the celebration of the liturgy at the Abbey and had spent both Christmas and Easter there for many years. Father Hirschmann writes that Edith confessed to him that she had a great devotion to her name, a singular love, for it contains the mystery of her conversion.

Her friends who attended the investiture were all struck by her transformation. Hedwig Conrad-Martius writes that Edith had always been childlike and amiable, but now she was enchanting in her childlike laughter and happiness. During my visits to the Cologne Carmel, I have spoken with nuns who lived with her and they remember her so. They remember especially her laughter. She said once to them, "I have never laughed so much during my whole life as I have these two years as a novice."

Her stories and humor enchanted the nuns, but, above all, they were struck by her humility, her modesty. She never referred to her importance in the outside world. And, over and over again, I have heard that Edith had a special gift for relating to people. She intuitively felt the state of mind of others and knew what they needed and how to encourage them. Her love and goodness were natural. She herself had a need to help other people.

I asked if she had shown signs of still being artistically inclined and received an enthusiastic "Yes!" She loved plastic sculpture and kept a silver Japanese vase in her cell by the Madonna; she had copies of paintings on cards (Rembrandt was her favorite); she had a great love for music, wrote poetry, and created little plays for the nuns' entertainment. The young lady who had so enjoyed dancing, hiking, boating, tennis, theater, concerts and literature was now content behind the cloistered walls.

She continued to do her intellectual work, which they believed was the fruit of her intense prayer life and devotion to truth. Her first endeavor was to write *Life in a Jewish Family*, for she had started this during the painful months at home before she entered Carmel. She writes in the Preface that she had a dual motivation: she wanted to honor her mother on whose memories she relied, and she wanted to present the true nature of Jewish humanity to the young Nazis being taught to hate Jews by way of a false stereotype.

Edith had a strong power of concentration and creative energy which the nuns attributed to her deep powers of prayer and contemplation; this enabled her to finish *Finite and Eternal Being* in nine months by giving up her free time and recreation. One of the high points of my visits to the Cologne Carmel was the discovery that Edith's translation of Psalm 61 is included in *Gotteslob*, the official prayer book used at all Masses daily in Germany: hymn #302.

Both nuns I interviewed at Cologne felt that Edith, in a deep fidelity to her people, wanted to experience their actual suffering. The Nuremberg Statutes were declared shortly after she took her first vows in 1935. Among many severe injunctions, Jews were deprived of all legal rights and marriages with Gentiles were forbidden. The following spring, 1936, the Nazis marched into the Rhineland.

This was a very hard year for Edith. Her mother died of cancer on September 14. It was the feast of the Exaltation of the Holy Cross and the day on which the nuns annually renewed their vows. Edith said afterwards, "As I was standing in my place in choir waiting to renew my vows my mother was beside me. I felt her presence quite distinctly."[46]

This is believable, given the special bond of love between them and Edith's intuitive power which was now developing in a mystical direction. Her sorrow was relieved by a special cause for rejoicing, for her sister Rosa came to her at Christmas and was baptized. She had been a believer for many years.

Because Edith as a born Jew had lost her right to publish, *Finite and Eternal Being* could not be published under her own name. It was proposed that the work be published under the name of a Nazi sympathizer but Edith refused. When the book finally did appear in 1950, it was acclaimed as invaluable towards a much needed rehabilitation of Catholic thought.[47] Aristotle, Plato, Duns Scotus, Thomas Aquinas and Husserl underlay the basis of her analysis, but her method was phenomenological. She herself explains in the opening of the book that she is attempting to contribute to a philosophical issue of much contemporary importance: the question of Being through an examination of the relationship between Thomistic and phenomenological thought.[48]

In March, 1938, Hitler invaded Austria and, in September, the Sudetenland. Edith's final vows were in April of that year. Her great trauma was now upon her. On Good Friday, she writes in a poem dedicated to the Virgin Mary—and Edith had an abiding, deep love for Our Lady—that those whom Mary chooses as companions must stand with her at the foot of the cross to purchase new life for souls:

> Today I stood with you beneath the Cross,
> And felt more clearly than I ever did
> That you became our Mother only there.
> Even an earthly mother faithfully
> Seeks to fulfill the last will of her son.
> But you became the handmaid of the Lord;
> The life and being of the God made Man
> Was perfectly inscribed in your own life.
> So you could take your own into your heart,
> And with the lifeblood of your bitter pains
> You purchased life anew for every soul.
> You know us all, our wounds, our imperfections;
> But you know also the celestial radiance
> Which your Son's love would shed on us in Heaven.
> Thus carefully you guide our faltering footsteps,
> No price too high for you to lead us to our goal.
>
> But those whom you have chosen for companions
> To stand with you round the eternal throne,
> They here must stand with you beneath the Cross,
> And with the lifeblood of their bitter pains
> Must purchase heavenly glory for those souls
> Whom God's own Son entrusted to their care.[49]

At the end of October, ten days before the fatal "Kristall-nacht," she writes in a letter that, like the Jewish Queen

Esther who was singled out from amongst the Jews to plead to the king for her people, she, also, will plead—to the heavenly king—for her own people.

We know the havoc of "Kristallnacht" on November 9th, when synagogues, Jewish homes and businesses were destroyed, and thirty to forty thousand Jews were sent to concentration camps which already existed as early as 1933. Edith and the nuns feared for each other's safety, and during the night of December 31st, she fled to the Carmel in Echt, Holland.

The Echt Carmel is a small, unpretentious row house in a quiet village. Last year, I saw her cell, held her Bible and saw her formal chapel cape. I asked the present prioress if she knew whether Edith had been melancholy there. "No," she said: in seclusion, Edith's face indicated she was lost in thought, but in the company of the nuns she was most cheerful and friendly.

And amusing anecdotes about Edith are tenderly remembered. She was unhandy at housework. Holding the broom in front of her and pushing it, she would walk up and down the room—just pushing it! The nuns would burst into laughter and that did not embarrass Edith in the least. Her sewing was so inadequate that when she finished working on something, like a little scapular, the prioress would take it quickly to another nun and tell her quietly to fix it!

Edith was in charge of professions and taught the novices Latin. But she was also concerned with the intellectual and spiritual advancement of the nuns who did the manual work. In those days, the nuns who did the gardening, cooking and laundering did not have library privileges; Edith asked that they be allowed to read good books and attend lectures. She did not succeed.

However, her poetry and other writings of this time show that, inwardly, Edith suffered much travail. It was clear during the days of 1939 that the world was heading for war. On January 30, Hitler declared that should the Jews cause another world war, they would bring about their own extinction. On March 25 he stated, "Poland should be totally subjected." The next day Edith wrote the following note to the prioress. It was Passion Sunday.

> Dear Mother, I beg your Reverence's permission to offer myself to the Heart of Jesus as a sacrificial expiation for the sake of true peace: that the Antichrist's sway may be broken, if possible without another world-war, and that a new order may be established. I am asking this today because it is already the twelfth hour. I know that I am nothing, but Jesus wills it, and He will call many more to the same sacrifice in these days.[50]

In June she wrote her last will. She concluded with a joyful acceptance of her death foreordained by God, for the sake of God's glory, the Sacred Hearts of Jesus and Mary, the intention of Holy Church, the deliverance of Germany and world peace, and for her family living and dead.

The Germans invaded Poland on September 1st, 1939. It was the beginning of World War II. A few weeks later on the feastday of the Exaltation of the Holy Cross, Edith wrote an impassioned essay, "Hail Cross, Our Only Hope." This former nurse of World War I reveals here a personal anguish in her inability to personally attend the wounded and dying and to console others in their misery. But she ecstatically affirms that there is an actual power of healing and consoling available even to the cloistered religious, for compassionate love and prayer is at one with Christ as He "soothes, heals and redeems."

The following lines from one of her poems reveal an agony alike to Christ's in the Garden of Gethsemane: "Bless,

O Lord, the sinking mood of those who suffer/The heavy loneliness of troubled souls/The restlessness of human beings in mortal pain/Which none would trust to tell a sister."[51]

In 1940, Edith's sister Rosa came to Echt and acted as portress for the nuns. She wanted to become a religious but instead became a third order Carmelite, for Hitler invaded Holland in May of that year. Starting on September 1st of 1941, both sisters were forced to wear the Yellow Star of David on which was inscribed the word "Jew."

They had to report periodically to the Gestapo. On one such visit, Edith greeted the officer with the habitual greeting of Catholic Germany: "Praised be Jesus Christ!" The officer stared at her but said nothing. She later explained that she had been compelled to do this, foolhardy as it could have been, because of her clear recognition of the eternal struggle between Christ and Lucifer.[52]

In an attempt to get Edith out of the country, the prioress applied to the Le Pâquier Carmel in Switzerland. However, they could take only Edith and she refused to go without her sister. This caused further delay. In time, arrangements were made for Rosa at a house for third order Carmelites near Le Pâquier. Now, all that was needed was authorization from the Dutch authorities.

Meanwhile, Edith was writing works of a mystic bent: *Wege der Gotteserkenntnis—Dionysius der Areopagit (Ways to Know God—Dionysius the Areopagite)*[53] and *Kreuzeswissenschaft (Science of the Cross)*[54], a study of the life, theology and poetry of St. John of the Cross. The spirituality described in a passage here was now hers: "Thus, the bridal union of the soul with God for which it is created is purchased through the cross, perfected with the cross, and sealed for all eternity with the cross."[55]

In her essays on Heidegger, Edith writes that metaphysics alone cannot explain the innermost life of the soul—only mystics like St. Teresa of Avila can do this. It is clear that Edith herself was a mystic as well as a philosopher.

And she was objective to the end as well. She was certainly not set on death although she was prepared for it: she writes that she is carrying on her person Matthew 10:23 which reads: "When they persecute you in one town, flee to the next."[56]

On July 1st, 1942 the education of Jewish Catholic children was forbidden in Holland by the Nazis: this meant the children could not attend Catholic schools, their only means of learning. The Dutch bishops protested this action as well as the deportation of the Jews in a pastoral letter on July 26th. In retaliation on August 2nd, the Nazi authorities ordered the arrest of all Dutch Catholics of Jewish descent. Edith and Rosa were among those picked up that evening. People, aghast, gathered at the door of the convent. The last words heard as the two sisters left the convent were Edith's as she said to Rosa, "Come, let us go for our people."[57]

They were taken to three camps during the next week: first, to two Dutch camps—Amersfoort and Westerbork; finally, to Auschwitz. Witnesses who survived the camps have testified to the holy love manifested by Edith.

Many of the mothers were in despair and had even given up caring for their own children:

> Sister Benedicta at once took care of the poor little ones, washed and combed them, and saw to it that they got food and attention. As long as she was in the camp she made washing and cleaning one of her principal charitable activities, so that everyone was amazed.[58]

She is described by a Dutch guard of Westerbork:

When I met her in the camp Westerbork I knew this was truly a great woman. She was in the hell of Westerbork only a few days, walking among the prisoners, talking and praying like a saint. Yes, that's what she was. That was the impression which this elderly woman gave, though, on the other hand, she seemed quite young. She spoke in such a clear and humble way that anybody who listened to her was seized. A talk with her was like a visit to another world.[59]

Edith was finally effecting Christ's ministerial action as He "calms, soothes, and redeems."

Months before, she had written the following:

I am quite content in any case. One can only learn a "Science of the Cross" if one feels the cross in one's own person. I was convinced of this from the very first and have said with all my heart "Hail Cross, our only hope."[60]

The Dutch Red Cross reported that the two sisters were in the transport which left Westerbork on August 7th and arrived at Auschwitz in the early hours of the 9th. We know the rest.

Footnotes

1. Teresia de Spiritu Sancto Posselt, *Edith Stein*, trs. Cecily Hastings and Donald Nicholl (New York: Sheed and Ward, 1952), p. 236.
2. *KL Auschwitz Seen by the SS*, ed. Kazimierz Smolen (Auschwitz: Panstwowe Museum, 1978), pp. 175-176.
3. *Ibid.*, p. 115.
4. Posselt, p. 12.
5. Edith Stein, *Aus dem Leben einer jüdischen Familie*, eds. Dr. L. Gelber and Fr. Romaeus Leuven, O.C.D. (Louvain: E. Nauwelaerts, 1965). The incidents described here are to be found in this autobiography of Stein's childhood and youth which has recently been published in English under the title *Life in a Jewish Family* (Washington, D.C.: ICS Press, 1986).

6. *Ibid.*, p. 90.
7. *Ibid.*, pp. 145-146.
8. Stein's own description of her student days at Göttingen can be found in chapter 7 of her autobiography *Life in a Jewish Family (Aus dem Leben)* and in chapter 3 of Posselt.
9. Hilda Graef, *The Scholar and the Cross* (Westminster, MD: The Newman Press, 1955), p. 15. This is Graef's own translation of her book that appeared earlier in German: *Leben unter dem Kreuz* (Frankfurt am Main: Verlag Joseph Knecht, 1954).
10. Hedwig Conrad-Martius, "Edith Stein," *Hochland*, 51, #1 (Oct. 1958), p. 40.
11. Elizabeth de Mirabel, *Edith Stein* (Paris: Editions du Seuil, 1954), p. 73.
12. Conrad-Martius, *ibid.*
13. Edith Stein, *On the Problem of Empathy*, tr. Waltraut Stein from *Zum Problem der Einfühlung* (The Hague: Martinus Nijhoff, 1964), pp. 20-21.
14. Adolf Hitler, *Letters and Notes*, ed. Werner Maser (New York: Bantam Books, 1974), p. 40.
15. *Aus dem Leben*, pp. 231-232.
16. See Roman Ingarden, "Edith Stein on Her Activity as Assistant of Edmund Husserl," tr. Janina Makota, *Philosophy and Phenomenological Research*, 23, #2 (Dec. 1962), pp. 155-161.
17. Graef, p. 24.
18. This writer was granted the courtesy of examining the letter of Father J. Hirschmann at the Edith Stein Archives in the Carmel of Cologne.
19. *Jahrbuch für Philosophie und phänomenologische Forschung*, Volume 5 (1922) and 7 (1925).
20. Hitler, p. 211.
21. Posselt, p. 64.
22. Conrad-Martius, pp. 38, 42.
23. See Chapter 11, "The Road to Carmel" in Posselt.
24. *Festschrift* Sankt Martin 1879-1979 (Bad Bergzabern: Katholische Pfarrgemeinde Bad Bergzabern, 1979).
25. John M. Oesterreicher, *Walls are Crumbling* (New York: Devin-Adair Co., 1950). See Foreword by Jacques Maritain, p. vii.
26. Graef, p. 54.
27. Rt. Rev. Msgr. Eugene Kevane, "St. Thomas Aquinas and Education," *The Catholic University of America Bulletin*, #4 (April 1961), pp. 2, 6. See Thomas Aquinas' *Q. disp. de Magistro* art. 1 and *Summa theol.* I Q. 12 art. 5.
28. See J.H. Kardinal Newman, *Gesammelte Werke*, eds. Daniel Feuling, O.S.B., Erich Przywara, S.J. and Paul Simon, tr. Edith Stein (München: Theatiner-Verlag, 1928-1933), Volumes 1 and 2.
29. *Edith Steins Werke*, eds. Dr. Lucy Gelber and Fr. Romaeus Leuven, O.C.D. (Louvain: E. Nauwelaerts and Freiburg: Herder), Volumes 3 and 4. Stein's *Works* will be designated below as *Werke*. Erich Przywara acknowledged his own debt to Stein and to Husserl in his Preface to *Ringen der Gegenwart* (Augsburg: B. Filser, 1929), Vol. 1, pp. 7-10. He attributed much importance to Stein's contribution to the relationship of Neo-Scholasticism and phenomenology. See particularly his "Neo-Scholasticism in Germany," *The Modern Schoolman*, Volume 10 (May 1933), pp. 91-92.

30. *Werke*, Vol. 2.
31. *Festschrift* Edmund Husserl zum 70 Geburtstag gewidmet (Halle: Niemeyer, 1929).
32. *Werke*, Vol. 5, *Die Frau* (1959). This was published in English in 1987 by the Institute of Carmelite Studies in Washington, D.C. as *Essays on Woman*.
33. *Ibid.*, pp. 96-97.
34. *Ibid.*, pp. 224-225.
35. *Ibid.*, p. 212.
36. Francis J. Lescoe, *Existentialism: With or Without God* (Staten Island: Alba House, 1974), pp. 176-178.
37. See "La Phénoménologie" in *Journées d'études de la Société Thomiste* (Juvisy: Les Editions du Cerf, 1932).
38. *Werke*, Vol. 2, p. 407.
39. Posselt, p. 117.
40. *Ibid.*, p. 118.
41. *Werke*, Vol. 2, p. 410.
42. Karol Wojtyla, *Faith According to St. John of the Cross*, tr. Jordan Aumann (San Francisco: Ignatius Press, 1981), p. 49.
43. Posselt, pp. 128-129.
44. *Edith Stein*, ed. Waltraut Herbstrith (Verlag Herder: Freiburg im Breisgau, 1983), p. 71.
45. *Ibid.*
46. Posselt, p. 168.
47. See Rudolph Allers, "Endliches und Ewiges Sein," *The New Scholasticism*, vol. 26 (1952), pp. 480-485.
48. *Werke*, Vol. 2, Introd., p. ix.
49. Graef, pp. 209-210.
50. Posselt, p. 212.
51. Waltraut Herbstrith, *Das wahre Gesicht Edith Steins* (Bergen-Enkheim bei Frankfurt/Main: Verlag Gerhard Kaffke, 1971), p. 169.
52. Posselt, p. 198.
53. Edith Stein, *Wege der Gotteserkenntnis-Dionysius der Areopagit* (München: Gerhard Kaffke, 1979).
54. *Werke*, Vol. 1.
55. Edith Stein, *The Science of the Cross: A Study of St. John of the Cross*, eds. Dr. Lucy Gelber and Fr. Romaeus Leuven, O.C.D., tr. Hilda C. Graef (Chicago: Henry Regnery Co., 1960), p. 241.
56. Graef, p. 225.
57. Edith Stein, *Briefauslese 1917-1942* (Freiburg: Herder, 1967), p. 136.
58. Graef, p. 229.
59. See Posselt, Chapter 7, "The Way of the Cross" for a coverage of Stein's arrest, imprisonment, and death.
60. *Briefauslese*, p. 127.

CHAPTER TWO

Edith Stein on
MARY AND TODAY'S WOMAN

It seems to me that we may think of Our Blessed Mother as the first Jewish convert. And so, with all due respect, I must admit that you have before you a Jewish convert writing about another Jewish convert who wrote about the original Jewish convert!

Certainly, no one can understand Mary without seeing her in her Jewishness. There is a painting by Delacroix which shows St. Ann guiding a small Mary's finger along the page of what is probably Scripture. Commenting on this painting, Jean Guitton asks:

> What does Mary read? Probably her own history, hidden under symbolic figures, the figures of the women or of the virgins of Israel, of Rebecca or of Eve, the "Mother of the human race" . . . And so does the Virgin, guided by her Mother, read dimly between the lines, her own destiny.[1]

How close Edith Stein must have felt to both Mary and Christ in their common heritage, what Vatican II's Declaration on the Relationship of the Church to Non-Christian Religions, *Nostra Aetate*, par. 4, calls "the spiritual patrimony common to Christians and Jews," what our beloved John Paul II has called "the sacred link" tying both faiths. She must have exulted in Mary's exultation over the coming Savior, the awaited Messiah, in the Magnificat:

> He has come to the help of his servant Israel for he has remembered his promise of mercy, the promise he made to our fathers, to Abraham and his children for ever (Lk 1:54-55).

Like every Jewish convert, Edith knew she was not forsaking Judaism but rather penetrating into it with greater fidelity.

From her early childhood Edith was made aware of the Jewish concepts of atonement and redemption. As mentioned in Chapter 1, she felt herself to be particularly dear to her mother for having been born on the Day of Atonement. And her mother always remained for Edith the image of the pious woman, an image which I do not doubt led to Edith's devotion to Our Lady, to her concept of Mary as the ideal woman and instrument of Christ's redeeming love.

This chapter will present Edith Stein's theology of Our Lady along three specific lines: Mary as Virgin, Mother and Co-Redemptrix. In each case, I will relate this to Edith's ideas on woman. My presentation is based on passages in her own works, especially *Die Frau (The Woman)*, *Endliches und Ewiges Sein, (Finite and Eternal Being)*, and *Welt und Person (World and Person)*.

Before doing so, however, it might be helpful (even at the risk of a little repetition) to present a summary of Edith's basic thought on woman.

The core, the key to woman, is to be mother and spouse, mother and companion. Let me stress that Edith's concepts of maternity and of companionship are not at all limited to the married state. This distinctive feminine nature belongs essentially to the woman in any role she may play—single, married or religious, and the education of woman should be such that she should be prepared to take on any of these roles. This supreme gift which only woman possesses is a beautiful and holy one. It goes out to everyone who comes into contact with her whether it be in family, public or professional life. It is the key not only to her nature but to her intrinsic value as woman.

The wife and mother acts in a complementary role to that of her husband: no competition is necessary for she complements the man as one hand does the other. Edith does ask that the woman recognize that there can be only one head of the family: therefore she should give the man a slight edge in authority! But Edith warns woman not to give up her prerogative as a person and always to retain her own judgment. Woman is to develop her own personhood for that is what is intended.

Edith was particularly concerned here with the Nazi oppression of women. She warns that it is most important that woman not surrender her entire being to any creature or try to surrender all her love to a creature, for only God can fulfill this total capacity for love.

Edith addresses a problem which has grown to monumental importance today: she does suggest that woman try to take care of her very young children herself. This is so for no one can actually replace her. If there is a real economic necessity for a woman to work during her child's early years, the person she chooses to look out for her youngster must be someone she can really trust. And never should she give up her divine privilege—her bond with her child.

On the other hand, Edith very strongly urges that women who are free to occupy themselves professionally should do so because they need interaction with an outer world: they need a give and take with other people on an objective level. Otherwise, they may become hyper-hysterical—she calls it "hyper-feminine"—because left on their own, women can get into a great deal of trouble!

Edith is particularly eloquent in speaking of the unmarried woman; one senses that she is speaking from her own interior depths. She writes of the virgin who is consecrated to Christ, her life totally given to His service. Her suffering becomes a fruitful death from which grace for others springs. Such a life which awakens and fosters the divine life in others is the highest and most sanctified vocation which a woman can have. However, this life is not only for the single woman, the consecrated virgin, the "Spouse of Christ." It can be shared by all women who share this function of spiritual maternity.

The heart of a single woman who is completely given over to Christ, dedicated to Him, and consecrated to Him in virginity overflows with a love for humanity. But this heart also finds love in the fullest measure for it is met with gratitude and reciprocal love in the hearts of other human beings yearning for magnanimous love. Such a yearning exists even in those estranged from God. And those already filled with love for Christ recognize each other and are united as children of God. A life spent in union with God can neither be lonely nor loveless. The unquenchable source of formation for the feminine heart is the Divine Heart which alone is able to lead each woman to her perfect fulfillment as woman.

This union with God and other creatures in God's love is vital in order to forestall an hysteria which may otherwise develop in the single woman. Because her body and soul are one, she finds more difficulty in fulfilling her role as woman than the married woman does. And Edith warns that the woman involved in professional life has to face the danger of overspecialization, which is also true of the man: she may become developed in one particular way at the expense of her formation as a full human being. All this can be prevented by an intimate relationship to God.

Edith writes that woman is especially receptive to God's workings in the soul. Her mission is to allow herself to become a flexible instrument in God's hand, His special weapon to combat evil. Woman is to be a healthy, energetic spore in a sick society. She is to resist the pressures from without by a self-containment within. She is to be quiet, warm, clear, empty of self, mistress of soul and body. Woman's unique value must be spent for the general good, for that which is of value today must be made fruitful for the community.

She is by nature created to do so, for woman possesses a driving force towards a total humanity for herself and for others. The man dedicates himself easily and objectively to a discipline and its precepts, but he often does so at the expense of his full humanity. However, woman's attitude is a personal one. Because she is emotion-centered and possesses a natural power of empathy, she is able to grow in humanity herself and to find ways to foster the personal relationships which help others to develop as human beings. For this reason woman is particularly effective in disciplines such as teaching, medicine, social work, law, and all public services. But, writes Edith, woman has a built-in, adaptive equipment which enables her to function in any job held by a man!

Suggesting that the attitude of the Christian woman through the centuries has been too passive, Edith cries out that the twentieth century demands that the Christian woman become involved in the burning issues of the day. Here she presents an unforgettable image of Our Lady:

> The example of Mary is relevant here. She is the ideal type of woman who knew how to unite tenderness with power. *She stood under the cross.* She had previously concerned herself with the human condition, observed it, understood it. In her son's tragic hour she appeared publicly. *Perhaps the moment has come for the Catholic woman also to stand with Mary and the Church under the cross.*[2]

Let us now see in more detail how woman can stand with Mary in her aspects as Virgin, Mother and Co-Redemptrix.

1. VIRGIN

St. Augustine's influence on Edith's work is perhaps as great as that of Thomas Aquinas. He tells us that the reason Mary was surprised at St. Gabriel's message is that she had already made a vow of virginity. Therefore, Edith writes, God had already instilled in Mary her consecrated vocation *before* the Annunciation. Her declaration of self as "the handmaid of the Lord" in answer to the strange news of motherhood reveals her utter trust in God and dedication to His service.

Both Christ and Mary were made free from that dependency of relationship to another human being for the fulfillment of life's significance. This is replaced by the relationship of each to God: Christ through the hypostatic union, Mary through total surrender. A new form of being is initiated, that of consecrated virginity which becomes another status in the redemptive order.

Whoever hears the call of Christ should grasp His hand, for even outside of conventual life, the consecrated virgin is the spouse of Christ. It is impossible for a life spent in union with God to be lonely and loveless; the virgin who lives and functions in society's mainstream will find love in others reciprocal to her own love for God and His creatures. Such women function in the marketplace as "an army of Christ."

There is a natural relationship between the nature of woman and the unique essence of religious life. It is specifically a feminine yearning to give herself completely to another as well as to be completely possessed by the other. When such self-abandonment is directed to a person instead of to God, it can easily become perverted because no human being can really fulfill that yearning. The German poet, Rainer Maria Rilke, puts it this way:

> Her [women's] devotion wants to be immeasurable; that is her happiness. But the nameless suffering of her love has always been this: that she is required to restrict this devotion.[3]

Only God can fully respond and yet lose nothing of Himself, which cannot happen in human relationships. The more one forgets oneself in this total commitment to God, the more God's life—the love of the Divine Heart—fills the soul. This life heals the sick and awakens the dead spirit within others as it cherishes, teaches, and forms. And this, Edith writes, is the motivation, principle and goal of religious life.

Virginity provides a natural goal for the education of young women because it is an authentic form of the feminine nature, one in accord with the divine image of womanhood found in Mary who constitutes the feminine form of the Christian image. Of course, as the first and perfect follower of Christ, she is pertinent to the formation of male Christians as well.

For Edith Stein, youth work, particularly the Christian formation of young girls, is the greatest challenge to the Church. She believes that girls have a great potential for the life of faith: the feminine nature has a special susceptibility to the works of God in the soul; there is a unity and tenacity within feminine nature, a tendency of total self-giving which is needed in the act of faith.

Only an early developed awareness of the mystery of Mary's virginity can enable a young girl to fight for her own purity. Understanding of Mary's union with God will enable her to make her own inner act of surrender. Introduction to Marian dogma is also an introduction to the concept of "the Spouse of Christ," of standing side by side with Him, and this is needed for Christian formation. If this were followed, there would arise a generation of mothers whose children would not be orphans. (Although Edith Stein was writing several decades ago, does this not speak for our predicament today?)

Edith based her analysis on her own educational work with girls and women at St. Magdalene's. It was during these years that she turned her attention to an analysis of woman's nature and vocation in order to formulate a proper approach to the education of women.

It is important to remember that Edith's own personality was transformed by her conversion. She had been quite a critic of human nature, always with laughter but yet at times with caustic wit. Now her students and colleagues found her to be gentle, patient, modest and humble, loving and lovable, serene and balanced, charitable and holy.

Throughout her work holiness is defined as the primary human vocation. In fact, surrender to the divine life within is the prerequisite for a full development of selfhood. God is the Master Educator and Sculptor of the person. Only the one who images Him can be a total human being, with his or her faculties fully developed and in harmony. Christ is the ideal human personality, its perfect Gestalt, combining the best characteristics of both sexes. (It must be noted that Edith Stein's full analysis of the person predated by several decades the contemporary absorption in this topic.)

Love, in the last sense, is only the surrender of one's own being and the becoming one with the beloved. Such surrender typified by Mary's "Fiat" is the strongest act of free will. The life of prayer depends on such surrender. The one who lives the interior life knows that he is drawn in a more compelling way to this inner life than he is to the outside world. The reward is the invasion of a new, powerful higher life—the divine life. We find God in ourselves.

Even artistic creativity is a fruit of "Hingabe," surrender. Every great genius is a mouthpiece through which God's voice wants to make itself heard. And each individual can find his own unique creativity, his pure development as a person, only if he is willing to trust in God's providence, to recognize its signs, and to surrender to it. Mary herself illustrates this in having chosen virginity, which was foreign to the tradition of her people. Each human being is unique. Thus, there is not one undifferentiated goal for all women.

The meaning and value of feminine differentiation is shown most significantly in Mary. She stands beside the new Adam, leading humanity to Him. She is the image of womanhood in the service of love which yearns to lead others to perfection. Edith herself is an exciting instance of Mary's pure womanhood. God drew her to Him in great love and she imitated Mary in her response of perfect surrender. In both, the Saint and the Queen of Saints, intellect, will and heart were set in perfect balance by love.

Edith writes that the intellect of Thomas Aquinas functioned on the highest level—that of pure Spirit. I believe this is true of Edith Stein. Her chasteness of mind and soul is unmistakable. A luminosity radiates from her writing, a clarity of mind which is achieved only by enlightenment of the Holy Spirit.

Edith is a writer of objectivity, a philosopher faithful to the sense of "the sacredness of being," "the purity of things, in themselves" which was characteristic of Edmund Husserl's early school of phenomenology.[4] In the face of today's skepticism regarding Mary as Virgin Mother, a skepticism which stems from pagan intellectualism and a corrupt lifestyle, the testimony of this pure woman—who is considered one of the great intellectuals of the twentieth century—is indeed inspiring.

Her conversion is wonderful in many ways. There is the wonder of a great intellect bowing in perfect humility and child-like trust to its Maker. She is able to refute Heidegger's negativeness concerning existence by a simple metaphor. She writes that in spite of momentary transitoriness ("Flüchtigkeit") which Heidegger makes so much of, she knows herself to be secure. She can abide in a state of confidence ("Sicherheit") like that of a child in the arms of its mother. Or would the child be reasonable, she asks, if it were always afraid that its mother would drop it? This metaphor appears in both Isaiah and the Psalms. Edith was a great lover of the Psalms and I would like to think that Psalm 131:2 is the source for her metaphor.

> Enough for me to keep my soul tranquil and quiet, like a child in its mother's arms.

2. Mother

I find particular joy in turning now to Edith Stein's views on the spiritual maternity of Our Lady. I was able to confess faith in Christ only after *first* being able to say "Mary, Mother of God." This was in the 3 p.m. daily recitation of the rosary with the late Father Gilbert V. Hartke at the Speech and Drama Department of the Catholic University of America.

Mary is the symbol of the spiritual maternity of the Church of which woman acts as an essential organ. The bridehood and maternity of the "Virgo-Mater" is continued, so to speak, in their maternity, and in their lives as brides of Christ. Mary collaborates with every woman wherever she is fulfilling her vocation as woman authentically. In imitation of Our Lady who leads all humanity to Christ, woman is called to advance human development and grace in every walk of life. As such she is a symbol of the Church. Our Lady stands with Christ at the crucial point of history. She is the Mother of the living, not because posterity comes from her physically, but because the Mystical Body of Christ is embraced by her maternal love. And she is the original cell of this body, the first to be sanctified by Christ and impregnated by the Holy Spirit. Edith writes, "Before the Son of Man was born of the Virgin, the Son of God conceived this very Virgin as one full of grace and God conceived the Church in and with her."[5]

"God conceived the Church in and with her." Does this sound too strong for sophisticated ears of today? Yet a 20th century French writer, Paul Claudel, poetizes the language of the Church in regard to Mary's Immaculate Conception. He writes that "occupying the principal place in the plan of Creation, she was ordained for all eternity before the earth was, and that when God was composing all things, she was there playing in a hundred reflections."[6] Of course this concept is part of traditional faith. The artist Diego Velasquez has depicted Mary as she appeared in the mind of God before Creation: She floats on the moon with the twelve stars of the Apocalypse about her.

In 1964, Mary was titled "Mater Ecclesiae," "Mother of the Church." In Vatican II's Constitution on the Sacred Liturgy, *Sacrosanctum Concilium*, par. 103, we read: "In her the Church holds up and admires the most excellent fruit of redemption and joyfully contemplates, as in a faultless model, that which she herself wholly desires and hopes to be."[7]

Let us return to Edith Stein. Just as Mary generates spiritual life, woman's primary mission is the formation of youth as cells of the Mystical Body of Christ. (In face of the suffering of our own youth, this is a very important message today: the despair among adolescents, so great that they actually turn to suicide; child abuse and child neglect; loneliness and fear which induce the use of drugs and alcohol, pornography, abortion—indeed, every form of violation of self as well as of the other.)

To win children for heaven is genuine maternity: it is the most exalted vocation for all women. To awaken divine sparks in a child's heart is a joy not of this world—to see the divine life develop in a child's heart or even the benumbed, frenzied soul of an adult separated from God. And Edith writes that the primary responsibility for children and youth belongs to the woman. The small person becomes a child of God in baptism, but she says: "Grace in the child is like a hidden little flame which must be painstakingly tended and nursed."

The mother has to lay a secure foundation for religious education or else the school has a hard time. It is because the woman has a special affinity for moral values that this

1. Edith Stein, Sr. Teresa Benedicta of the Cross (1938)

6. (l-r) back row: Frau
Platau, Frau Dorothea
Biberstein, Frau
Auguste Stein (Edith's
mother); middle row:
Rose Guttmann, Paul
Berg, Erna Stein, Hede
Guttmann, Elfriede
(Frieda) Stein
Tworoger; front row:
Edith Stein, Lilli Platau
(the baby is Erika
Tworoger, Elfriede's
daughter), Rosa Stein

7. (l-r) back row:
Sophie Mark, Frau
Guttmann, Edith
Stein; middle row:
Erna Stein, Rose
Guttmann, Lilli
Platau; front row:
Hans Biberstein

8. Edith Stein
(seated, left end of
the table) as a Red
Cross nurse at the
Mährisch-
Weisskirchen
hospital for
contagious diseases,
1915

4. (l) Erna Stein; (r) Edith Stein

5. Edmund Husserl

2. Family portrait of the Stein family (1895); (l-r) back row: Arno, Else, Siegfried (father), Elfriede (Frieda), Paul; front row: Rosa, Auguste (mother), Edith, Erna. Edith's father Siegfried died in 1893. His picture was superimposed on this photo.

3. The Stein family's house in Breslau (now Wrocław)

14. Edith Stein during her year at the German Institute of Scientific Pedagogy at Münster, 1932-33

11. Auguste Stein (Edith's
mother), c. 1925

13. Edith Stein, c. 1925

12. Edith Stein, c. 1925-1930

9. Edith Stein, c. 1916

10. Edith Stein with a nephew
(1921)

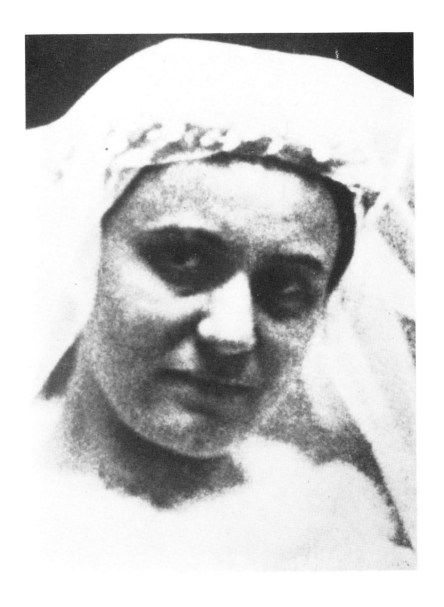

15. Edith Stein at her religious vestition, April 15, 1934

responsibility is hers. Children can understand the transcendental nature in the Incarnation as well as in the mystery of the Mother of God, and it gives them an insight of what a trusting union can mean in their lives.

When a child is separated from its mother in the formative years, it cannot easily learn this trust in God and develop the confidence, the caring attitude necessary for a harmonious adjustment to the world. Only a child who knows himself safe in his mother's love develops such trust and considerateness. The teaching of value judgments and a sense of responsibility towards others must be instilled early.

It seems we have to take this to heart because the concept of responsibility is disappearing in many ways. The Nazi mentality of an Adolf Eichmann is not unique. He cried out during his trial:

> I obeyed. Regardless of what I was ordered to do, I would have obeyed. Certainly, I would have obeyed. I obeyed. I obeyed.[8]

Finally, he said "Yes . . . I must bear the responsibility."

The mother must bring the child to a willingness to exercise self-autonomy which endures pressure and which functions responsibly in the Body of Christ. We will see shortly that it is this sense of mutual responsibility which constitutes the nature of the Church as Community.

Our Blessed Mother is the prototype, the ideal of all authentic womanhood by virtue of the fact that the essence of spiritual maternity belongs inherently to the very nature of woman.

To do so, woman's soul must be magnanimous, open, quiet, warm, clear, self-contained, empty of self, mistress over itself and body. This is the ideal for woman's soul. Only the souls of Eve and of Mary were formed so in original nature, but there is in all other women an embryo for such development through grace and education.

I think we might agree that this description of the ideal feminine Gestalt does not fit the image of the modern woman. The painful statement of the Dominican Walter Farrell comes to mind: "There is nothing in an age that so sharply mirrors its philosophy as the lives of its women."[9] Today, many would have us believe that due to changing times, woman's nature is changing and hence her destiny as well. Edith Stein would refute that. Humanity, she writes, is a dual species, masculine and feminine, which cannot be changed by varying circumstances and factors.

Helene Deutsch, the famous psychologist, asks an interesting question: "Are women meant to be faithful by nature?" and she answers, "Yes, because violations of her sacredness of person through promiscuity brings her only unhappiness in the long run."[10]

Of course, this is Edith's view as well. And she has developed an ontology of woman which presents cosmic and eternal truths because she faithfully describes woman's nature, role and destiny as created by God. To do so, she incorporates Holy Scripture and Church tradition. She was an ardent feminist, and she cautions that an authentic feminist movement must adhere to the eternal truths of faith. The Catholic Women's Movement of her day *was* accepted by the Church, and she was its "voice," its intellectual leader.

Her lectures on woman, now collected in her book *Die Frau*, were delivered in the major cities of Europe from 1928-1932.

It is impossible to present fully the sexual ethics and moral theology contained in this book. Contemporary studies are only now beginning to offer what she wrote then. She was perhaps 100 years ahead of her time. Most basic to her analysis is the acuteness of her mental and spiritual powers.

She establishes the basis of healthy sexuality and person-hood in marriage, professional life and religious life. She affirms the benefits of marriage as offspring, conjugal fidelity and sacrament, declaring that upon Catholic theology alone can marriage survive as an institution. She relates the young woman who wants to stay home with her child to Mary caring for Jesus in His dependency.

But she believes that woman has a mission in society as well as in the home, for in all professional and public life she is to serve God in her fellow creatures. Woman is challenged to stamp her unique feminine nature on her activity. This can only be an asset to those around her since the essence of her nature is her spiritual maternity.

Edith has some interesting observations concerning woman on the job. She must be "the handmaid of the Lord." To do so, she goes about her work as quietly, discreetly and unobtrusively as Mary did at Cana. If she sees what is needed and remedies the situation without trying to put herself in the limelight, she will be a good spirit. In fact, if Mary's ethos is preserved, the professional woman can only bless society.

Woman has a special power for good in public life because she is God's instrument of love to fight evil. Mary appeared publicly in the most dramatic confrontation between good and evil: the Crucifixion. The modern Catholic woman must become involved in the burning issues of the day and be familiar with the needs of the masses. She is not just a "Co-sufferer" but, as a member of society, she is "a jointly responsible member of the entire nation," supplying healthy energy to the entire national body if she herself is a whole person. Edith Stein's unsuccessful attempt to get Pope Pius XI to condemn the persecution of the Jews is an example in her own life of such involvement.

Also most essential to an understanding of her emphasis on responsibility is her belief that Christ is the head of all humanity and therefore, that all humanity forms the Mystical Body of Christ. She develops this concept at the end of *Finite and Eternal Being*, written in the 1920's and 30's, years before the Church stressed the concept at Vatican II.

Edith was very devoted to the Church and faithful to it. She asks, "What is the Church's view of women?" and answers very objectively from four aspects: dogma, canon law, the hierarchy and Christ Himself. A personal tone is sounded when she reminds us that in the early Church women carried on various apostolates as martyrs and consecrated deaconesses, and when she hopes that women will be called upon more and more for works of charity, pastoral activity and teaching. The Church needs woman-power, she declares; therefore *Christ* needs them. The call to Catholic action was issued to both man and woman.

Is there a difference in the call of God sent to man and woman? It is from the attitude of Christ Himself that her final assessment comes concerning priesthood for women. Although Mary, Queen of Apostles, excelled all others by grace and human perfection, she was not granted the status of priesthood by Christ. Nor were any of the women who were among His disciples and closest friends included. Yet, there was no difference in Christ's *manner* to men and women. Indeed, His love and grace showered in such abundance on women indicates that He is calling them more and more to Church duties.

In one passage she does wonder if the rising demands of women to be included in ordained Church ministry may after all be the first step in their way to the priesthood. The Church does endure through the centuries because of its ability to harmonize unconditional eternal truths with the challenges of changing times. But, in other passages, she

reiterates that she does not think the question can be re-
solved in the passage of time other than in keeping with
Christ's initial choice of men as priests.

3. Co-Redemptrix

Edith writes that women like Mary who can forget
themselves completely in prayer, contemplating Christ's
passion and participating in His redemptive action, can
change the history of the Church and the world. When she
lost her position at the German Institute for Scientific
Pedagogy in the spring of 1933, she decided after 13 hours
of straight prayer to finally become a religious. She chose
Carmel because she believed that this order excels in a free
and joyous participation in Christ's redemptive action. She
wrote that only the Passion of Christ can save the world and
she wanted a share in this. What is most striking is that her
intention of redemptive suffering was to share in the suffering inflicted upon the Jews. She wished this not only because
she *was* a Jew, and she *did* suffer for them; but she also
believed that their suffering is a continuation of Christ's
crucifixion throughout time. And she believed herself to
have been *chosen* for this role, as Queen Esther of old, to
plead to the heavenly King for her people.[11]

Edith's redemptive role is unique in its duality, yet she is
very much like Mary who suffered as a Jew and as the first
Christian. And it is Mary as Co-Redemptrix who shows us
the path of human participation in Christ's redemptive
action.

Edith is known to have knelt for many hours before a
picture of Our Lady of Sorrows. A picture of Edith was
taken before she left the Carmel in Cologne and traveled to
the Dutch Carmel in Echt in order to escape Hitler. There is

an expression on her face of deep pain and sorrow, human sensibility and compassion, and yet perfect serenity and control. It is reminiscent of Our Lady depicted in a painting by Mathias Grunwald, "Virgin Supported by St. John": there is the same "nobility of suffering and . . . nobility of peace."[12]

She stood with Mary beneath the cross. In notes and testaments she offered her prayer and life itself to the Immaculate Heart of Mary and the Sacred Heart of Jesus. She prayed for the welfare of the Jews, Germany, the Church, world peace, and her family living and dead.

Now, I know it is not stylish today to refer to Mary as Co-Redemptrix, but that is exactly the way Edith saw her. Mary is, Edith writes, our entry to the redemptive order. The language in John Paul II's encyclical *Redemptor Hominis* is very similar. Mary is described as providing "the point of entry into the divine and human dimensions of the mystery of redemption in Christ."[13]

Edith writes that Mary replaces Eve as the true Mother of the living because she is the first fruit of the reversal from fallen to redeemed nature. For all humanity, she wins victory over evil, fulfilling the prophecy of Gn 3:15, "I will put enmity between you and the woman, between your seed and her seed." This is the origin of Edith's image of woman as God's instrument of love fighting evil. The feminine nature has a unique characteristic of empathy, and in addition to her concern for the person, she has a special sensitivity for moral values.

St. Paul tells us (1 Tm 2:5-6): "For there is only one God, and there is only one mediator between God and mankind, himself a man, Christ Jesus, who sacrificed himself as a ransom for them all." We believe that redemption was won for us once and for all at Calvary. Yet Catholic theology upholds our Lady as mediatrix: she is midway between us and God by grace and spiritual maternity; she is holiness itself; she intercedes for us.[14]

Edith extends the concept of mediation to all the Mystical Body of Christ which, as already said, embraces all of humanity. In an essay "The Ontological Structure of the Person," she asks if one human being can be mediator for another. She concludes, yes, the more a person is filled with divine love, the more qualified that person is to intercede for others. The mediator appeals to God to grant the movement of grace and contrition in the sinner's heart and to apply the possible merits of the one praying to the one prayed for. But she goes further, incorporating the mediator's prayer into redemptive action. There is the possibility that the mediator can choose freely to act as proxy for the sinner, asking to receive the suffering due in justice for the sin of the other.

She writes that each person is responsible, certainly, for his own salvation, but "each person is at the same time responsible for the salvation of all others insofar as he has the possibility of begging for grace for those others through his prayers." Because grace can come to a human being *indirectly* from God, i.e. through another human being, prayer of intercession becomes a matter of communal concern. We intercede for another, but even more, by the love for our neighbor in God, his salvation becomes our concern. This dynamic, driving love becomes the authentic, healing power of prayer.

Christ alone incarnates the fullness of God's love and for this reason is the *only* proxy of all humanity before God. He is the true head of the *community* incorporated in the Church. All other members of the Church are imperfect and intercede for each other according to their capabilities. It is just for this reason that we *need* each other. "One person for all and all for one constitutes the Church."

She concludes that God grants a person grace if He draws him as proxy to compensate for others through suffering. A deep religious meaning thus penetrates conditions of injustice.[15] It is my conviction that in the acknowledged prayer for Germany, Edith offered herself as proxy for the sins of the Nazis. This is the answer of a saint for the problem of forgiveness concerning the Holocaust. She describes the redemptive power of Christ in the faithful as "that formative life-giving power which we have called *The Science of the Cross.*"[16]

The saint only practices what Christ asks of all of us. St. Paul tells us (Col 1:24): "I am glad of my sufferings on your behalf, as, in this mortal frame of mine, I help to pay off the debt which the afflictions of Christ leave still to be paid, for the sake of His body, the Church." Frank J. Sheed discusses this teaching in a lovely essay, "The Com-Passion of Our Lady." Mary, he writes, was intended for suffering in order that all of us should learn from her to unite our sufferings to Christ's redemptive action. He writes, "it was in the glorious design of God that human love should not be denied all place in the expiation of human sin, with men condemned to be no more than spectators of their own redemption."[17]

Survivors of Auschwitz have testified to Edith's heroism and holiness as she constantly cared for the women and children physically and consoled them spiritually. Witnesses have described her as "a great woman," "a Saint," "a Pieta."

Edith Stein was beatified in May of 1987. Not the least part of her claim to this honor is her true imaging of Mary in her own life and the relevance she bestows on us of Mary in *our* lives. She heralds and deepens the new understanding of unity between Jews and Christians. With Mary, she is a sign of that unity. But through her life and writing, all of us are called to that conversion and reconciliation which our

Blessed Mother may be beseeching through the young people in Medjugorje in Yugoslavia. On the Jewish Holy Day of Atonement, the shofar is blown, announcing freedom from sin and a new birth of life. We are blessed by the sacrifice of Edith Stein. And then, it is no small thing for a Jewish girl to be beatified. No doubt, the Mother of Divine Grace approves.

Footnotes

1. Jean Guitton, *The Madonna* (New York: Tudor Publishing Co., 1963), pp. 16-17.
2. *Edith Steins Werke*, eds. Dr. Lucy Gelber and Fr. Romaeus Leuven, O.C.D. (Louvain: E. Nauwelaerts and Freiburg: Herder), Vol. 5, *Die Frau* (1959), pp. 25-26. This was published in 1987 in English translation under the title *Essays on Woman* by the Institute of Carmelite Studies in Washington, D.C.
3. Rainer Maria Rilke. *The Notebooks of Malte Laurids Briggs*, tr. M.D. Herter Norton (New York: W.W. Norton and Co., 1949), p. 176.
4. Hedwig Conrad-Martius, "Edith Stein," in *Edith Stein Briefe an Hedwig-Martius* (München: Kösel-Verlag KG, 1960), pp. 62-63.
5. *Werke*, Vol. 5, p. 190.
6. Paul Claudel, *A Poet Before the Cross* (Chicago: Henry Regnery Co., 1958), p. 83.
7. *Documents of Vatican II*, ed. Walter M. Abbott, tr. Joseph Gallagher (New York: Guild Press, 1966), p. 168.
8. *Eichmann Interrogated*, eds. Jochen von Lang and Claus Sibyll, tr. Ralph Manheim (New York: Farrar, Straus and Giroux, 1983), p. 198.
9. Walter Farrell, O.P., "Our Lady and the Status of Woman" in *The Mary Book*, ed. Frank J. Sheed (New York: Sheed and Ward, 1950), p. 373.
10. See "Eroticism and the Feminine Woman" in *The Psychology of Women* I (London: Research Books Ltd., 1946).
11. Letter of October 31, 1938 in *Werke*, Vol. 9, p. 121.
12. Guitton, p. 110.
13. See the analysis of *Redemptor Hominis* given by Rev. Augustine DiNoia, O.P. in a talk "Christ the Measure of Man" at the College of the Immaculate Conception in Washington, D.C. This talk is part of the 1983 series of the St. Catherine of Siena Colloquium on Spirituality; it is available on tape through Ministr-O-Media in Pomfret, Md.
14. *New Catholic Encyclopedia*, IX, p. 359.
15. *Werke*, Vol. 6, pp. 161-68.
16. *Werke*, Vol. 1. This is available in English translation: *The Science of the Cross*, tr. Hilda C. Graef (Chicago: Henry Regnery Co., 1960).
17. Frank J. Sheed, "The Com-Passion of Our Lady" in *The Mary Book*, p. 239.

CHAPTER THREE

Spring of the Bitter Valley:
EDITH STEIN
and
THE HOLOCAUST

"As they go through the Bitter Valley/ they make it a place of springs." These are lines from Psalm 84 in the New American Bible. In the Jerusalem Bible, the phrase "the Bitter Valley" reads "Valley of the Weeper" and "Valley of Tears." And certainly, as the victims of the Holocaust went through their bitter valley, they wept much.

But yet, this is "A Song of Pilgrimage," the title given by the Jerusalem Bible. The psalmist is celebrating faith in the human heart where God dwells. It is this indwelling which enables the pilgrim, as he journeys to the heavenly Zion, to turn his bitter valley into a place of springs.

How lovely is your dwelling place,
Lord, God of Hosts.

They are happy, who dwell in your house,
for ever singing your praise.
They are happy, whose strength is in you,
in whose hearts are the roads to Zion.

As they go through the Bitter Valley
they make it a place of springs,
the autumnal rain covers it with blessings.
They walk with ever growing strength,
they will see the God of gods in Zion (Ps 84:2, 5-8).

Many who went to their death in the Holocaust gave witness to this absolute faith. The Jewish people called upon "Yahweh," "Redeemer," "the Holy One of Israel" (Is 41:14).

Let us also remember the Christians who witnessed to their faith in their resistance to National Socialism. We know of Maximilian Kolbe, Dietrich Bonhoeffer, Titus Brandsma and Edith Stein. These names are well-known, but there are so many of whom little or nothing is said.

When the Nazis took over in 1933, they immediately dispersed the existing Youth Movement. These young people remind us in many ways of our own idealistic youth in the 1960's: they wanted to build a better world—a new world—based on new values. From this movement came important resisters.[1]

Hans and Sophie Scholl were arrested for dropping protest leaflets, "The Pamphlet of the White Rose," from a balcony onto the lobby of the University of Munich. Alexander Schmorell wrote before his execution: "This whole terrible 'misfortune' has been necessary to show me the right way. For what did I know before this of faith, of true deep faith, of truth, of the ultimate and only truth of God?" Another member of this group, Christoph Probst, wrote: "Never before have I felt so powerfully the indestructibility of love."[2]

In France, a young man not yet twenty, Robert Busillet, wrote in prison on Christmas: "I lack nothing, and that which I ask of God is not put into shoes; it is received into the heart."[3] A deeply moving testimony of great beauty is a letter by a Dominican tertiary, Dr. Ruth Meirowsky, in which she wrote: "Join me in giving thanks to God for having chosen me and sing a jubilant Magnificat."[4] These letters are all last testaments.

Edith Stein was another opponent and victim of the Nazis. She had no illusions at all about the depth of their evil. She called Hitler the Antichrist and tried—unsuccessfully—to get Pius XI to condemn the Nazi persecution of the Jews. And yet she included the Nazis among the people she prayed for.

The Holocaust is a terrible mystery. We wonder, like Job, how God could let such terrible things happen. Edith Stein's ideas on evil and vicarious atonement, coming as they do from a beatified Carmelite who was both a Jew and a victim of Hitler, give us a unique perspective on this mystery.

When Edith wrote that woman is to be God's instrument against evil, she was thinking of evil as a driving, living entity, an actual spirit and power. She describes evil as "a being opposed to its own original nature and direction of being," hence, a perverted being going in a negative direction, away from God.

This may seem to echo somewhat St. Augustine's *City of God*. Yet, in her work *Finite and Eternal Being*, she refutes his arguments on evil as well as those of Pseudo-Dionysius the Areopagite and Thomas Aquinas. She suggests two basic errors in their thought: first, failure to recognize the dualism in man, the two autonomous sources which he initially receives—a good and a bad one; secondly, failure to recognize that evil can be traced back to God because He is the only source of all being. She writes:

> If evil is not a being then these two difficulties can be surmounted, and that is why the Christian theologians have mustered all acuteness in order to demonstrate that evil is neither an autonomous Being, nor something in a being, nor any manner that a being could have. It seems to me, however, that these efforts to differentiate between a mere natural defect (like a born weakness of intellect) and actual evil (for instance, the misuse of the "good" intellect for bad purposes)—this has not been satisfactorily developed. The theological distinction between punishment for sin and punishment for evil is concerned with this, but in the metaphysical discussion, the contrast of both kinds of evil disappears in the summary under the label of non-being.[5]

It seems to me that the saint, the holy one of God, has always recognized that human misery is caused by human sin. It stands to reason then that if the perversion of the human will, the turning away from God, brings about disorder followed by misery, then a total surrender to God must earn love, peace and perfect human fulfillment.

Edith was fighting with the power of prayer. As all contemplatives, she believed with Dionysius the Areopagite that "The divinest of all divine work is to co-operate with God in the salvation of souls"; such work is the "fruit of union" with God; it imitates God's work in its greatest glory.[6]

She had that divine mission which holy souls have: an overwhelming desire to share in the Passion of Christ. Many times she voiced her belief that only Christ's Passion can save humanity. On Passion Sunday of 1939, a few months prior to the outbreak of World War II, she wrote a note to her prioress offering herself to the Heart of Jesus as a vicarious sacrifice for true peace.

I offer now a few concepts from her essay "The Ontological Structure of the Person" which she wrote on vicarious suffering. It explains her intentions beautifully. We have already touched on this in our consideration of Mary as Co-Redemptrix, but it is appropriate here to give this subject some further attention.

She terms her concept of mediation and intercessory prayer "Stellvertretung." Literally, this means "taking the place of another," language which goes back to that used in her doctoral thesis on empathy. In Steinian terminology, the "Stellvertreter" acts as proxy for the guilt incurred by the other person who sins. Here I suggest that Edith was actually taking upon herself suffering incurred by the guilt of the Nazis. We can only view this as a perfect participation in Christ's redemptive action.

She builds her concepts on the teachings of St. Thomas Aquinas regarding satisfaction. He writes in the *Summa Theologica, Summa Contra Gentiles,* and *De Veritate* that one friend can make this satisfaction for another as long as both are in a state of charity. He tells us that man is indebted to God for favors received and does receive reward for his merits. This merit, he writes, one man cannot transfer—one man does not merit the essential reward for another.

Edith writes that it is possible to implore that one's reward for merit be ceded to another. Of course, this is the proxy's free gift of petition that God will permit the sinner to attain the grace he needs. She writes:

> And God can, for love of a soul which he has taken up for Himself, draw another person to Himself. That the divine freedom submits Himself to the wishes of his

chosen ones at the time that He listens to prayer is one of the marvelous facts of the religious life. Why this is so goes beyond all comprehension.[7]

In this appeal for grace for another, she is simply developing Aquinas' teaching that grace precedes contrition, that grace is needed for the sinner's free movement of will.

Now in the matter of satisfaction for guilt incurred by the sinner, St. Thomas holds that love between two people in friendship makes them one: therefore, one man can merit for another in regard to release from punishment. One man's act actually becomes another's by means of charity, for both are one in Christ. This becomes the Steinian concept of "standing in as proxy" in the passage under discussion. The "Stellvertreter" prays for a turning away from sin by the sinner and takes upon himself the suffering due to the other. But, and this is the wonderful thing, she says "Do it for friend and enemy." Here Edith makes a unique contribution on a cosmic level. She writes that the possibility of such intercession makes salvation a *communal concern*. Because each person has the opportunity to effect grace for another through prayer, it is apparent that each person is co-responsible for another who has not yet attained grace. As such, he shares the guilt for every sin which another has laid upon himself. When a proxy offers himself, he is only doing at the present time what he has previously omitted doing. Each person is responsible in prayer not only for his own salvation but for all others. This concept of one person for all and all for one constitutes the Church as Community.

The more a person is filled with divine love, the more he is uplifted to act as proxy for another, for prayer is grounded in love. Here, following Aquinas, she writes that Christ is the total fullness of love and therefore the only proxy for all humanity. Others are imperfect and render services according to their talents, and it is just this reason that we need each other.

Edith has been consistently using the concept of acting as proxy "for one's neighbor." The question arises if she is using this phrase within the identical context of Aquinas. I believe she is not. Aquinas writes:

> . . . in the case where one is bound to look after the salvation of his neighbor, he is also bound to expose his bodily life to dangers for the sake of that salvation. But this is perfect charity, that he also expose his bodily life to dangers for those to whom he is not bound as to a neighbor.[8]

Edith offered up both her prayer and her life for others' salvation and fulfills Aquinas' definition of perfect charity. But she believed that *all are bound to all as neighbor.* All. Aquinas' words are "if you give up your life for those to whom you are not bound as to a neighbor" but Edith writes that all are bound to all as neighbor.

I can't help thinking that when Edith sat with her mother in the synagogue (even after her conversion, she continued to go with her mother to keep peace), she often heard the verse, "Thou shalt love thy neighbor as thyself" (Lv 19:13). We may ask, then, what is Edith's concept of "neighbor"? She answers us in an essay, "The Mystery of Christmas":

> For the Christian there is no stranger. Whoever is near us and needing us must be "our neighbor"; it does not matter whether he is related to us or not, whether we like him or not, whether he is morally worthy of our help or not. The love of Christ knows no limits. It never

ends; it does not shrink from ugliness and filth. He came for sinners, not for the just. And if the love of Christ is in us we shall do as He did and seek the lost sheep.[9]

Edith was still at the Cologne Carmel when she wrote this, but after the disastrous pogrom on November 9, 1938—the infamous "Kristallnacht"—the nuns were aware that they must get Edith out of the country for her sake as well as for the good of the convent. On the last night of 1938, she was rushed to the Dutch Carmel in Echt.

Here she writes *Kreuzeswissenschaft (The Science of the Cross)*, and, interestingly enough, she has not given up her concept of neighbor. Working within the context of the theology of St. John of the Cross, she is still able to write: "It is an obvious truth that sympathy with one's neighbor grows in the measure that the soul is united to God by love." Also, zeal for souls is the fruit of union with God, and love for our neighbor is a means to such a union.[10]

A natural reaction to this concept would be the difficult question of loving an enemy such as the Nazis, especially if one suffered under them. Edith has an answer for that, too. She writes in *Finite and Eternal Being*, "Holy souls who are determined to confidently maintain a courageous love for their enemies have experienced that they have the freedom to so love." Where does such power come from? Participation in Christ's redemptive action gives that power which *is* the science of the cross.

Such a power of love to stand in place of the sinner implies a complete self-giving, and this is a manifestation of the divine life, the triune God within ourselves. She writes: "Since the Creator is the prototype of creation, should there then not be in creation an image, though ever so distant, of the three in one of original Being?" The self-giving of creatures is a reflection of the self-giving of the three divine Persons. She continues, "The more recollected the person lives in his innermost soul, the greater the power he radiates outwardly and the greater the influence he exerts on others." Indeed, it is only the one who does live in the temple of his interior being who has the spiritual strength necessary to confront the world and it is this strength which influences others.[11]

Therefore, man must enter into himself to find God and eternal life. "If we do not find God, we do not find ourselves and the spring of eternal life that is waiting for us, within us."[12]

We have come full circle, back to the human heart celebrated in Psalm 84.

Edith had received the full impact of the baptismal spring of grace. I find great beauty in the antiphon of the Feast of Christ's Baptism: "Springs of water were made holy as Christ revealed His glory to the world." And I relate this to the voice that spoke over the waters of the Jordan and recollect that it is the same voice of God that sounded over the primeval chaos of the deep in the moment of creation. Having been an adult at the time the sacrament was conferred, I know that in baptism we are pulled out of that deep, primeval darkness by waters made holy at the Jordan in the meeting of Father, Son and Holy Spirit.

Edith knew the reality of her transformation, and she gives herself so that we, also, can be transformed. She writes that if she had only one thing to say, it is to live in the hand of God. As we are all called to do, she had become another Christ. Her faith in God was absolute.

The one who does the will of God learns to know the divine spirit, divine life, divine love—in other words, God Himself. For, in surrendering fully to what God

wants of him, the divine life becomes his inner life; in
contemplation, he finds God within himself.[13]

I stress her faith here because, as Alfred Delp writes,
"modern man had lost his susceptibility to God." This Jesuit
philosopher-theologian pleads that all human effort must
be directed to making man once more susceptible to his
Maker; there must be a passionate mission concerning humanity, "a passion of faith, of dedication, of striving, of
service." To do so one must remain interiorly free of exterior forces and conditions. Otherwise, one is lost. Himself
an outspoken witness to the faith, Delp was executed by the
Nazis in 1945.[14]

What can we learn from the death of the saints "so
precious in the sight of the Lord"? How can we survive and
help each other in this Bitter Valley existing today, this
Holocaust? Edith died at Auschwitz in 1942. There is a line
in a little book titled *Christus im Konzentrationslager (Christ in
the Concentration Camp)* written by a witness, Leonard
Steinwender: "The blood of martyrs is the seed of new
Christians."[15] This, of course, is a quotation from the *Apol-
ogy* of the 2nd century Christian writer Tertullian. But it is
true for the martyrs of the concentration camp as well as of
the Roman arena. Can we in some way get this passion of the
martyrs?

Fr. Delp had cried out in the face of all the injustices and
the silence of the German hierarchy, "Has the Church
forgotten to say 'No'?" Pastor Bernhard Lichtenberg of
Berlin did not keep silent but protested early in 1938 when
the great synagogue was set afire during "Kristallnacht"; he
said ". . . that also is a house of God."[16] This old priest was so
outspoken in his protests and prayers for the Jews that he
was arrested and sentenced to two years in prison. Instead of

being freed afterwards, he was sent to Dachau and, on the way, he died.

Yet, the same violence exists all about us. Statistics show a bitter reality: every day in our country, five teenagers commit suicide; every year, a million and a half abortions; thousands of children missing yearly; the terrible breakdown of family life in divorce; child neglect and abuse; loneliness; mental illness; the terrible havoc wrought by drugs and alcohol—violence of every kind inflicted upon oneself and one's neighbor.

The following words of Edith Stein seem very true for us today:

> Millions of children today are homeless and orphaned, even though they do have a home and a mother. They hunger for love and eagerly await a guiding hand to draw them out of dirt and misery into purity and light. How could it be otherwise than that our great holy mother the Church should open her arms wide to take these beloved of the Lord to her heart? But for this she needs human arms and human hearts, maternal arms and maternal hearts.[17]

A little German Jewish girl, Anne Frank, a few months before her death, wrote: ". . . I can feel the sufferings of millions and yet, if I look up into the heavens, I think that it will all come right, that this cruelty too will end, and that peace and tranquillity will return again."[18] This was written on July 15, 1944. She was arrested during August and died in February at the Bergen-Belsen Camp.

These noble spirits were instruments of our redemption. They were proxy for us. They give meaning to the Holocaust. Many Jews went to their death singing "Sh'ma Yisroel Adonoi Elohenu Adonoi Ehod!" ("Hear, Oh Israel, the Lord our God, the Lord is one!"). And Edith Stein, thirty years before the Second Vatican Council, insisted that all people are included in the Mystical Body of Christ.[19]

Let us return to the psalmist, and this time I would like to give the verses from the Jewish edition of the Old Testament:

Happy is the man whose strength is in Thee;
In whose heart are the highways.
Passing through the valley of Baca
they make it a place of springs;
Yea, the early rain clotheth it with blessings.
They go from strength to strength,
Every one of them appeareth before God in Zion.

(Ps 84:6-8)

Footnotes

1. See appendix "The German Youth Movement" in Ida F. Görres, *Broken Lights*, tr. Barbara Waldstein-Wartenberg (Westminster, Md.: Newman Press, 1964).
2. *Dying We Live*, ed. Helmut Gollwitzer et al, tr. Reinhard C. Kuhn (New York: Pantheon Books, Inc., 1956), p. 53.
3. Louis Aragon, *Le Crime Contre L'Esprit (The Crime Against the Spirit)* (Paris: les Editions de Minuit, 1944), p. 15.
4. *Dying We Live*, p. 233.
5. *Edith Steins Werke*, eds. Dr. Lucy Gelber and Fr. Romaeus Leuven, O.C.D. (Louvain: E. Nauwelaerts and Freiburg: Herder), Vol. 2, *Endliches und Ewiges Sein (Finite and Eternal Being)* (1950), pp. 371-73.
6. Edith Stein, *The Science of the Cross: A Study of St. John of the Cross*, eds. Dr. Lucy Gelber and Fr. Romaeus Leuven, O.C.D., tr. Hilda C. Graef (Chicago: Henry Regnery Co., 1960), p. 215.
7. *Werke*, Vol. 6, *Welt und Person* (1962), p. 161.
8. St. Thomas Aquinas, *On Charity*, a translation from *de Caritate* by Lottie H. Kendzierski (Milwaukee: Marquette Univ. Press, 1960), p. 93.
9. *Selected Writings of Edith Stein*, tr. and ed. Hilda C. Graef (London: Peter Owen Ltd., 1956), pp. 25-26.
10. Stein, *The Science of the Cross*, p. 215.
11. Stein, *Endliches und Ewiges Sein*, pp. 308, 405, 410.

12. Amata Neyer, O.C.D., *Edith Stein: A Saint for Our Time*, tr. Lucie Wiedenhoer, O.C.D. (Darlington: Discalced Carmel), p. 44.
13. Stein, *Endliches und Ewiges Sein*, p. 410-11.
14. *Dying We Live*, pp. 135-51.
15. Leonhard Steinwender, *Christus im Konzentrationslager* (Salzburg: Otto Müller, 1946), p. 50.
16. Guenter Lewy, *The Catholic Church and Nazi Germany* (New York: McGraw-Hill Book Co., 1964), p. 284.
17. Werke, Vol. 5, *Die Frau* (1959) p. 203.
18. Anne Frank, *The Diary of Anne Frank* (London: Pan Books, 1954), pp. 218-19.
19. Stein, *Endliches und Ewiges Sein*, p. 482.

CONCLUSION

Edith Stein once wrote, "I have an ever deeper and firmer belief that nothing is merely an accident when seen in the light of God, that my whole life down to its smallest details has been marked out for me in the plan of divine Providence and has a completely coherent meaning in God's all-seeing eye."[1]

Without trying to speak for God, what can we understand as the meaning of her life? First I see her as a symbol of the inherent unity between Judaism and Christianity and as a hopeful sign of their ensuing reconciliation. Indeed, St. Paul tells us that Christ has already reconciled Jew and Gentile by the Cross, creating from both a new humanity in His peace.

And I believe that God is working through her to affirm this reconciliation. I believe that through *her* passion, He is creating a resurrection of the human spirit and of brotherhood. St. Augustine tells us that Christ's Resurrection was God's supreme and wholly marvelous work. To rise, He had to die and so it is with Edith. I see her martyrdom as making wonderful things happen.

The Holocaust was a death of the human race. Edith stands for the ten million people who were consumed in the flames of the crematoria: six million Jews and four million Christians. We must pray that this fire of purgation will cleanse both faiths and put an end to their hostilities, effecting a redemption of all humanity.

And Edith believed that Christ's redemptive action is for all people, that all humanity is in some way included in the Mystical Body of Christ.[2] Each person is a unique revelation of God and is to be honored so. Hence, forty years before the Second Vatican Council, she declared that she cannot believe that salvation depends on the exterior limits of any Church. She becomes a symbol, then, of universal dimensions because she points to that universal realm of brotherhood above all barriers of nation, race and religion.

Edith wanted a share in Christ's redemptive action and she teaches us to assume a similar role. Each person, she writes, is co-responsible through prayer for the salvation and redemption of the many who comprise the human community.[3] She incarnates the essence of holiness itself.

And because she is a model of holiness, she becomes a model of human spirituality. Edith was a true Jewish heroine as well as a saintly Christian. She pitted herself against the forces of evil like the great Hebrew women we find in Scripture: Deborah, Ruth, Esther, Judith and Mary. Of course, she is specifically a model of Christian spirituality and holiness. For us Christians, she reveals the truths of our faith not as mere abstractions but as experiential, passionately lived truths which teach and heal us by their very organic power.

Edith is one with Christ because she went His way of the Cross. She gave herself totally to His ministry of love and reparation on earth. She believed that love conquers hate and evil, and that it is the Cross which is the sign of that victorious love because hate cannot triumph over the love inherent in self-sacrifice. The Cross is triumphant because it wins the redemption of the world.

This salvific power is desperately needed by society as a whole, and, surely, God grants us saints just when we need them! Edith Stein shows us the way out of our contemporary materialism, secularism and paganism through the power of love and prayer. In this day when technical science has become a God and is throttling the human spirit, she demonstrates that the search for truth is guided by the Spirit of truth and that, indeed, the love of God surpasses all knowledge. She presents a viable balance of reason and faith. That is why Peter Wust wrote of her, "A bride was led to the altar whose life might be taken as a symbol of the intellectual movement of the last decade."[4]

Finally, she has a mission to strengthen women, to help them find their full humanity as persons and as women. I have spent the greater part of my adulthood preparing to bring Edith Stein to the public because I know she is the model from whom we can all learn.

There is a difference between the giving of self for love of God and the unbalanced, abject surrender of some modern women enslaved by their passions. Rare among women, she was a philosopher, a highly successful professional as well as a holy woman. She must in some way help us to find the true way towards our mission as God's special instruments of love to fight evil.

Edith Stein reveals the beauty of God as Creator of humanity because of her own beauty. His beauty is in her. His intention of woman as a vehicle of divine love is fulfilled in her. She *is* the image of God. She manifests His qualities of self-giving, goodness, forgiveness, purity, holiness. She is another Christ.

She shows us the person of full humanity. Over a hundred years ago, Abbé Constant wrote that when women unite themselves to intelligence and love, they will give birth to a divine race.[5] Edith Stein was such a woman—God's lovely instrument. His love and intelligence are in her, in all her writings, in all her deeds to uplift the human race. Please God, we will be worthy of her sacrifice.

Footnotes

1. Waltraut Herbstrith, *Das wahre Gesicht Edith Steins* (Bergen-Enkheim bei Frankfurt/Main: Verlag Gerhard Kaffke, 1971), p. 147.
2. *Edith Steins Werke*, eds. Dr. Lucy Gelber and Fr. Romaeus Leuven, O.C.D. (Louvain: E. Nauwelaerts and Freiburg: Herder), Vol. 2 (1950), p. 482.
3. *Werke*, Vol. 6 (1962), pp. 161-162.
4. Teresia de Spiritu Sancto Posselt, *Edith Stein*, trs. Cecily Hastings and Donald Nicholl (New York: Sheed and Ward, 1952), p. 47.
5. L'Abbé Constant, *L'Assomption de la femme* (Paris: Aug. le gallois, 1841), p. 4.